BRINGING ITALY HOME

BRINGING ITALY HOME

CREATING THE FEELING OF ITALY IN YOUR HOME ROOM BY ROOM

CHERYL MacLachlan

WITH BO NILES

PHOTOGRAPHY BY
BARDO FABIANI

FROM THE BRINGING IT HOME™ SERIES

CLARKSON POTTER/PUBLISHERS
NEW YORK

To Fred,

FOR SHOWING ME THAT SPRING REALLY DOES FOLLOW WINTER.

ALL MY LOVE,

Cheryl

PUBLISHED BY CLARKSON POTTER/PUBLISHERS,
201 EAST 50TH STREET, NEW YORK, NEW YORK 10022.
MEMBER OF THE CROWN PUBLISHING GROUP.

RANDOM HOUSE, INC.
NEW YORK, TORONTO, LONDON, SYDNEY, AUCKLAND

CLARKSON N. POTTER, POTTER, AND COLOPHON ARE TRADEMARKS OF
CLARKSON N. POTTER, INC.

MANUFACTURED IN CHINA

DESIGN BY DONNA AGAJANIAN

LIBRARY OF CONGRESS CATALOGING-IN-PUBLICATION DATA
MACLACHLAN, CHERYL.
BRINGING ITALY HOME / BY CHERYL MACLACHLAN.—1ST ED.
INCLUDES INDEX.

1. INTERIOR DECORATION—ITALY.   2. HOUSE FURNISHINGS—ITALY.   3. COOKERY,
ITALIAN.   TITLE.

TX311.M2354   1995

645'.0945—DC20   94-42660

ISBN 0-517-59807-8

10 9 8 7 6 5 4 3 2 1

FIRST EDITION

ACKNOWLEDGMENTS

I would like to express my deepest gratitude to the people in Italy who welcomed me into their lives and shared the thoughts that ultimately added so much texture to these pages:

Francesca Antinori
Bianca Arrivabene
Donnatella Asta
Giovanna and Gisella Baquis
Marino and Marina Barovier
Nally Bellati
Bette Ann Bierwirth
Simonetta Brandolini
Giuliano Bugialli
Riccardo Caracciolo
Shirley Caracciolo
Judy Carter
Alessandro Corsini

Cino, Aimee, and Desideria Corsini
Carlo Di Perotti
Tia Raggi DiVencentis
Alessandro Falassi
Fiamma di San Giuliano Ferragamo
Francesco Giuntini
Marina Giusti del Giardino
Francesco and Eugenia Griccioli
Lino, Matteo, and Luca Lando
Katrina and Gianni Mannocci
Katherine Price Mondadori
Vittorio Mosca
Valeria Ossoinack

Sergio, Rosanna, and Alessandra Pezzati
Piero Pinto
Sabine Pretsch
Alessandro Pucci
Laudomia Pucci
Anna and Maria Giulia Ratti
Gianfranco Stoppa
Vincenzo Sugaroni
Cristiana Vannini
John and Judy Vestey
Angelica Visconti

To my Italian friends in the United States: Maurizia Bettazzato, Pietro and Claudia DeCamilli, and Giancarlo Masini, for their unique insights. And to my Italy-loving friends: Dori Cismowski and Eric Jones, Judy and Mel Croner, Lucilla Delforge, Wendall Harrington, Marsha and Michael Lasky, Shira Mayer, Patricia and Patrick Pera, and Connie Wiley, who helped in so many ways.

A very special thanks to Carlo Ducci, who knows everyone who ever lived in Italy and put me on the right path countless times, and to Ned and Tracy Bonzi, who shared every great spot they uncovered during their two years in Italy and gave me the guest room in Santa Margherita.

Bringing Italy Home was created simultaneously with *Bringing France Home*—an enormously humbling task that serves as dramatic testament to the fact that no writer is an island. I was blessed with much help and support and wish to extend my thanks:

To Nan Talese for her encouragement and help on this project while it was still in the "notion" stage, and to Gay Talese for his heartening remarks and support when I first showed him some of my writing.

To the "team": Bardo Fabiani, whose interpretation of "Nessun dorma!" remains my favorite and whose beautiful photographs fill these pages; Bo Niles, whose extensive knowledge of architecture and decoration and whose lovely way with words allowed her to take my manuscripts for both books and imbue them with precision and grace; Annetta Hanna (who came into the world only hours after me and thus must share a certain cosmic relationship with me), who skillfully edited, carefully tended, and vastly improved these books; Howard Klein, Clarkson Potter's Art Director, whose wonderful talent and vision is exceeded only by his patience and diplomacy; Donna Agajanian, a gifted designer who embraced both text and photography and made them dance together; Jane Treuhaft, whose computer I envy and who adroitly led the design of both books to a handsome conclusion; Jeff Stone, my agent and on-line inspiration who has been there for me since the start, and his partner, Kim Johnson Gross, for her always helpful advice; and finally, Lauren Shakely, Clarkson Potter's Editorial Director, who believed in me and my concept for this series.

CONTENTS

INTRODUCTION

Nearly ten years ago, I took my first trip to Italy. My colleagues from *Esquire* magazine and I were paying a visit to the president of a top fashion company in Milan during that city's biannual fashion market week. The hour neared twelve-thirty and the showroom buzzed with activity. Being sensitive to the time and fearing we had already overstayed our welcome, I thanked him and suggested we be on our way. He looked stunned. "You won't stay for lunch?" he asked. Understanding this as my cue to be polite, I answered: "Oh, we couldn't possibly, you have so much work to do."

The next ten seconds were to bring me into contact with a world for which my life in Manhattan had not prepared me. "If you leave," he said in no uncertain terms, "you insult me."

Certainly the last thing we wanted to do was insult him! We were welcomed into a bright kitchen, seated around a table set in white porcelain, and treated to a wonderful lunch of pasta, veal, salad, and fruit. Wine was poured during the meal and espresso was served after. "So," he said, all smiles and good cheer again, "we've had a nice lunch, we've shared some stories, and now we go back to work with plenty of time to finish our day."

What a concept.

I spent the rest of the week absorbed by the possibility that, even as a career woman with a demanding job, I didn't have to live the never-take-a-break life so accepted in big-city America. The follow-ing year I assumed the responsibility for the Milan, Paris, and London offices of *Esquire*, which not only gave me the opportunity to return to Italy frequently, but to become a keen observer of Italians and of Italian life. Italians are a fascinating people: vibrant, passionate, warm, sensual, and exquisitely stylish. My regular travel permitted me the luxury of making friends, spending time in private homes, relaxing over long dinners, and absorbing the texture and flavor of daily life. I found myself trying to distill the composite of the Italian lifestyle into its essential components, which, I reasoned, I could reassemble when I was back home.

Why not bring a country home?

Consciously or unconsciously, we are always affected by the people we meet and the places we see. That which stirs us positively—the way a friend makes risotto, the music at last night's concert, the combination of teal and cranberry on the armchair at the antique show, for example—we interpret and incorporate into our own lives.

Bringing Italy Home was written to give you access to the myriad little details that make Italy Italy. It does not assume you have devoted years of your life to the study of architecture, interior design, or regional cuisine. I focus instead on the more immediate questions: Why do Italian rooms look so elegant? Why is the food so delicious? Why does one feel so warmly welcomed? And, through these images, you'll learn how to re-create in your own home the aspects of Italian life that most appeal to you.

OPPOSITE: A dazzling display of glass crafted in Murano decorates the table in designer Piero Pinto's Venice home. Pinto restored the brick-and-marble structure, which had formerly been a chapel, adding a large gridiron floor to create a second level.

How to **Use** This **Book**

If someone asked you to describe yourself in a paragraph or two, you might make some generalizations that, although true, did not quite represent the full range of your character. You have many moods, many talents, many ways in which you express yourself.

Similarly, it is a challenge to describe the lifestyle of a country in one volume. Italy's enchanting personality emerged from its unique history: the powerful influence of Roman culture; the unparalled legacy of the Renaissance, set amidst a network of independent city-states, each with its own dialect and customs; centuries of invasions and annexations by the Austrians, the French, and the Spanish; and finally, in 1861, the creation of the Republic of Italy. It is a rich, diverse, and beautiful land, and indeed, from the breathtaking splendor of the Roman Coliseum to the surreal beauty of Venice, Italy's regional charms have graced the pages of countless volumes.

I have instead chosen to focus on the common threads that unite the various regions and styles of Italy. These pages are limited only to those elements of life in Italy that are transportable. It is those elements, in effect, that define the difference between incorporating aspects of Italian style into our lives and the mistaken belief that it is possible to "become Italian."

Bringing Italy Home is constructed like a house. After a brief overview of the qualities that give an Italian home its unique appeal, the book is sectioned into rooms, where we will look at the physical characteristics as they appear in both traditional and contemporary interiors. Where such aspects overlap—the way a window is dressed, for example—the subject is treated only once. Beyond the look of a room, however, we examine the way life is lived within its walls: how guests are entertained, how a meal is served, how a great cup of coffee is made, to mention a few examples.

Throughout *Bringing Italy Home*, and particularly in the Voices sections, you'll meet some of the men and women who welcomed me into their homes and shared their thoughts about everything from the importance of family to accommodating unexpected guests for dinner. Additionally, you'll find sections labeled From the Artisan's Hand, which provide a background and description of Italy's stunning handcrafted wares. In the kitchen chapter, for example, you'll learn about the wonderful terra-cotta tile made in a small village in Umbria.

Every effort was made to avoid clichés and to faithfully represent the passion for living that makes the Italians so spontaneous and irresistible. In that regard, *Bringing Italy Home* is not a set of rules—nothing could be more *un*Italian. Re-create or interpret anything that strikes your fancy. Consider this book a chance to stroll around town, meet the neighbors, and be welcomed inside their homes. Just don't suggest leaving before lunch.

THE
SUM OF ITS
PARTS

TO ENTER AN ITALIAN HOME, grand or humble, is to witness an instinctive elegance born from centuries of daily contact with some of the greatest works of art and architecture known to the Western world. From their earliest days, Italians are immersed in a world where proportions are always balanced, where colors enhance but never overpower, and where superior craftsmanship is not the exception but rather the standard.

The weathered stucco of "Lo Sbarcatello," a residence in the town of Porto Ercole, harmonizes perfectly with the terra-cotta urns and stone drive.

Graced with this innate sense of beauty, Italians create homes that, while possessing the signature of the individual family, share many common threads that make them *molto italiano*.

A SENSE OF **SPACE**

Two thousand years ago, the Romans became focused on "interior" design, as opposed to the exterior design that had so enthralled the Greeks. The Greeks reveled in the outdoors: their social and political discourse, athletics, and theater all took place under the open sky. Their temples, based on columns and the lintels that straddled them, were striking from the outside, but, confined by the span between columns, dense and cramped inside.

The Romans, by contrast, cared less for the outdoors. Although they too had open-air forums, they wanted indoor spaces where they could indulge their larger-than-life passions, where they could eat, drink, sing, talk, and enjoy the good life. The Romans developed the engineering to span space on a grand scale; their invention, the arch, virtually exploded space and made possible the capacious interiors with vaulted ceilings that allowed the Romans full expression

A beveled glass top placed upon two cornices provides a display for a stunning ceramic urn, while maintaining a light, spacious feeling in front of the large picture window. The owner's numerous periodicals and books temporarily occupy the table, waiting for filing day, when they will be systematically arranged in the library.

of their energetic and hedon-
istic delights: the baths at Ca-
racalla are just one example.

Over the centuries, the
Romans—now Italians—
never lost their appreciation
for space. Unlike the homes
of France and England, which
are cozy and often cluttered,
Italian interiors today appear
wide-open and, to some eyes,
even stark. In the Italian
home there is room to
breathe. One enjoys the luxury of moving easily around
pieces of furniture. The sofas,
loveseats, and club chairs
comprising a seating group
may be placed as much as
seven or eight feet from one another.
Long stretches of wall continue uninterrupted by tables, consoles, or other furnishings. Corners remain empty.
Kitchen counters are pristine, nearly
devoid of utensils. In short, Italians
express no desire to fill up empty spaces,
but instead luxuriate in the tranquillity
of their emptiness.

This sense of space reflects the
Italians' innate belief that, as Mies van
der Rohe stated succinctly, "Less is
more." Rooms are generally furnished
with just a handful of high-quality pieces.
It is not unusual, for example, to find a
bedroom containing only a bed and a
dresser, both impeccably crafted. In
many contemporary homes, much of the
furniture is built in: a sleekly designed
headboard encompasses night tables as

ABOVE: Two striking red couches placed parallel to one another enjoy not only the warmth of
a fire, but plenty of leg room. A kilim covers a
rough-textured terra-cotta tile floor. As in many
Italian homes, no coffee table stands between
the sofas.

TO CREATE A SPACIOUS FEELING, EVALU-
ATE YOUR CURRENT FURNISHINGS WITH A
CRITICAL EYE. ARE THERE CHAIRS, SMALL
TABLES, OR LAMPS THAT DO NOT RECEIVE
REGULAR USE? COULD THEY BE REMOVED
TO CREATE MORE UNOBSTRUCTED SPACE?
ARE THERE TABLE DRAPES, PICTURES, OR
OBJECTS DISPLAYED THAT YOU ARE NOT
REALLY IN LOVE WITH? OVER THE YEARS
WE TEND TO ACCUMULATE MORE CLUTTER
THAN WE REALIZE, AND, IN FACT, THERE
MAY BE QUITE A BIT OF SPACE IN YOUR
HOME FOR YOU TO RECLAIM.

LEFT: A beautiful marble-topped dresser is unencumbered by other furnishings in this peaceful bedroom in Orvieto. BELOW: An elegantly minimalist corner is created in this Rome apartment with a simple wrought iron table, a single chair, and an impressive canvas. The white marble floor provides a classic counterpoint to the dark grays and blacks of the furniture and artwork. *Photo by Genovese/Stylograph*

well as lighting; a floor-to-ceiling cherry wall unit serves as both dresser and closet; seating is constructed as a suede-cushioned platform with storage below. With so many functional items accounted for in this manner, floor space is freed up to provide plenty of room to circulate.

Beyond the basic preference for breathing room, the Italian interior owes its characteristic spaciousness to a firm belief that if a piece is well designed and well made, it can and should stand on its own.

Logically, then, furnishings from different periods may coexist within a room. Because each has a definite identity, an eighteenth-century credenza, for instance, will work well with a pair of nineteenth-century side chairs and with a contemporary sofa. Add to the mix a minimalist halogen lamp or two, an antique tapestry, or a lovely collection of glass objects, and the room coalesces into one elegant and harmonious whole.

SMOOTH
SURFACES

Sensualists to the core, Italians find smooth, polished materials utterly irresistible, and the objects of their desires are often sleekly surfaced. In the home, for example, floors, whether made of wood, marble, or tile, are meticulously maintained to keep their shine. Tables are rarely draped; their tops, crafted perhaps of shimmering bits of mosaic or multihued marquetry, seduce the eye with their light-reflecting clarity. In contemporary homes, glass, steel, and chrome are favored for the sheen they impart to the interior.

The appreciation for refined, sleek surfaces, however, goes beyond just the materials used. It is reflected in the phrase *tutto nascosto*—"everything hidden." Enamored of invention and ingenuity, Italians use the phrase with pride to remark upon something that is cleverly disguised or camouflaged. For example, a built-in wall system with invisible hardware and all-but-invisible joinery might be constructed to conceal a stereo, television, or bar. Such smooth, unbroken lines are especially appreciated in the kitchen, where, for most Italians, the ideal cabinet system has no visible hardware, but instead relies on spring latches or finger-hold indentations. Even the burners on the stovetop are to be covered. Many ranges are sold with a hinged steel lid that can be lifted for cooking and then lowered back to its horizontal position when the stove is not in use.

ABOVE: The surface of the dining table is polished to a brilliant shine in this Tuscany home. The table will be covered only at mealtime. RIGHT: Exquisite Murano glass from the private collection of gallery owners Marino and Marina Barovier is arranged on their beautifully maintained piano.

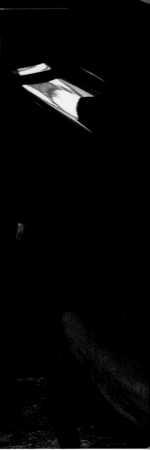

NOBLE
MATERIALS

Perhaps the next time you are searching for a compliment to describe how wonderfully constructed something is, you might consider saying it is built like an Italian home. The Italians have long been renowned for their skill in masonry and construction. Little wonder that engineering marvels such as the aqueducts and *colossea* of Roman design and the grand stone *palazzi* erected during the Renaissance still stand. Even many *case coloniche*, or humble farmsteads, bear dates that were incised into their walls centuries ago.

The structural integrity of the Italian dwelling is due not only to the skill of the craftsmen who built it, but to the noble materials used in its construction. Floors are laid with hardwood, marble, slate, limestone, or terra-cotta. Walls are composed of stone or brick, often sheathed in stucco; interior walls are beautifully finished in plaster, or with colorful ceramic tile. Balustrades are of lyrically curved wrought iron. Countertops are rendered in smooth granite, travertine, or tile. In short, Italians invest in the bones of a house before they consider its complexion.

Because the quality of materials used in construction is so fine, many Italians

OPPOSITE: The commanding presence of a black marble floor, with inlays of white marble, gives a distinctly elegant tone. *Photo by Sancassani/ Stylograph* LEFT: Architect Alessandro Corsini used a lyrically designed wrought iron screen for this New York apartment. *Photo by I. Terestchenko*

choose not to cover floors with carpeting, blanket walls with artwork, or crowd their interiors with accessories. They prefer to highlight the natural beauty of their interior surfaces.

The solid integrity of the Italian home is echoed in its furnishings and appointments. Tables and consoles, for example, will often support granite tops upon hefty fruitwood or wrought iron bases. A thick stone or marble pedestal may be capped with a solid piece of beveled glass, and oversized ceramic tiles often punctuate the stone surrounding a fireplace.

Top right: A magnificent *pietre dure* coffee table features a variety of semiprecious stones. Right: A rustic harmony is achieved between the rough terra-cotta floor, the weathered oak table, and the wrought iron chair. Bottom right: Angelica Visconti's wedding day is captured in the photos displayed atop a *pietre dure* table. Far right: Handsome marble stairs.

The strategic use of veneer and objects made of stone, tile, marble, and wrought iron can enhance the feeling of noble materials in your home. A fireplace mantel and surround can be resurfaced with marble. Architectural salvage yards often contain treasures that can be integrated into the interior. For example, a section of a wrought iron balcony railing can be covered with a piece of glass and made into a dining table or coffee table top, and two same-height stone cornices can be used as table bottoms.

Intermezzo
WEAVING
MAGIC

Although not generally considered a "noble material," as would be marble or wrought iron, Italy's fine silks are luxuriously regal. Indeed, in Renaissance Italy the nobility took pains to pose for their portraits dressed in and surrounded by their finest cloths in order to convey their wealth and status.

Ironically, the high esteem in which the Renaissance Italians held their fabrics led to ill-conceived efforts to control their consumption. Beginning in 1472 and continuing into the next century, Venice and other cities established sumptuary laws to dissuade people from overconsuming luxury goods. Silk, a perennial target of these strictures, was forbidden for such uses as window and wall hangings and for the presentation of newborns. And in Florence, an evangelistic Dominican reformer named Girolamo Savonarola preached extreme forms of austerity, culminating in his famed "bonfire of the vanities" in 1494; his fires were fed in part with costumes made of elaborately woven fabrics.

Fortunately for the sake of refinement and good taste, these attempts failed to dampen the enthusiasm for luxury fabrics. Today, Italy continues to weave some of the finest luxury fabrics in the world.

Luxurious silk jacquards and silk taffetas woven on nineteenth-century looms spill onto an old wooden cutting table in the showroom of Antico Setificio Fiorentino.

SECRETS
OF EXQUISITE
FABRICS

The Antico Setificio Fiorentino (the Old Florentine Silk Factory) is located in Florence's San Frediano section, the neighborhood that has quartered the city's artisans for centuries. The proprietor, Alessandro Pucci, and the general manager, Sabine Pretsch, gave me a tour of the silk factory, which was founded more than 200 years ago and which still operates exclusively with wooden hand looms and iron mechanical looms that predate the Industrial Revolution. It is the last of its kind in Italy.

Stepping onto the weaving floor at the Setificio is a heady experience, not unlike walking onto an impeccably decorated set of a period film. Strands of fine silk, illuminated by dappled sunlight, glisten on the old looms while the steady chatter of bobbins and shuttles fills the air. As I enjoyed the enchanting atmosphere, I asked Pucci and Pretsch for a lesson in discerning the difference in quality between an artisanally woven fabric costing from $100 to $1,000 a yard and a less precious fabric. They focused on four important points.

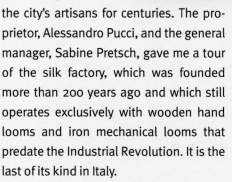

ALL SILKS ARE NOT CREATED EQUAL

Silk is known as the jewel of all fibers because it does not have to be altered by man in any way. The silkworm spins a cocoon from which a single strand of silk will be unwrapped. Artisanal fabrics are made only with top-grade cocoons, which yield flawless, evenly spun silken strands capable of absorbing dye so purely as to produce a true, consistent color in the finished cloth.

Individual fibers, or ply, are twisted together to make a stronger thread. The finest possible thread—which requires careful handling during the spinning and weaving processes—is two ply. Pretsch explained, "The natural shape of a silk fiber is triangular. Thus, it is capable of reflecting light from three faces, making a very luminous cloth." On modern, high-speed twisting machines, however, the silk fiber is subjected to so much tension, its triangular shape flattens into an elliptical shape that is much less capable of reflecting light. The surface of many silk fabrics is therefore treated

Two-ply threads of the highest quality silk are woven on a pre–Industrial Revolution loom to create a fabric sumptuous to the touch but also highly durable.

with a chemical finish to restore the luster that is lost in the spinning. A much "colder" light results from this process.

"Our threads are spun so slowly that the silk fiber is never subjected to excessive tension, thus it holds its triangular shape," said Pucci. He reached up to a bolt of silk, unfolded a meter, draped it across a nearby table, and then scrunched it into a ball. "Do you see how the light will bounce from every curve?" Indeed, the fabric seemed alive with a warm light. "And do you also see how the silk holds whatever shape I push it into?" Because the fiber has not been flattened by the spinning machine and is free from any chemical finish, the silk is thicker, denser, and has a richer body than would a lesser-quality fabric.

ARTISANAL WEAVING REQUIRES LENGTHY TRAINING

A quality fabric, Pretsch continued, is precisely and flawlessly woven. The weavers at Setificio, trained for a minimum of five years before they can master the loom, carefully watch for even the smallest imperfection. These generally result from one of two causes. One of the warp threads (there can be from 8,000 to 34,000 threads of silk in the warp) can break, which the weaver will spot as a tiny break in the fabric. She must stop the loom and trace the warp thread back to

locate and repair the broken strand.

The second risk of imperfection lies in the precision of the "repeat," the overall pattern in the fabric that repeats roughly every half meter to a meter (a meter measures approximately thirty-nine inches). If a single repeat is off by even as little as one centimeter, at the end of five meters the pattern will be off by five centimeters, making it virtually impossible to match up along seams for draperies and upholstery. A trained weaver is sensitive to the working of the loom and continues to make fine adjustments during the weaving process to ensure the symmetry of the pattern.

THE WEAVING PROCESS MUST RESPECT THE THREAD

In order to work with the very finest two-ply threads, Pretsch explained, the loom must be prepared and operated very carefully. Hand looms and the extremely

rare, pre–Industrial Revolution mechanical iron looms used at Antico Setificio are distinct in two ways: the warp threads, which run lengthwise, are joined by hand and the looms run very slowly. This means that the fibers are never subjected to the kind of stress that would necessitate using a thicker ply or a more tightly spun thread. With a two-ply thread, a finer weave is attainable, creating a fabric that is as durable as it is beautiful.

ARTISANS WORK PERSONALLY WITH THEIR CLIENTS

Lastly, Pucci addressed the personalized nature of artisanally produced fabrics, comparing the process to the small shops of yesteryear: "The client comes in; we have coffee; we discuss his or her needs and then we customize the colors, patterns, and trimmings required. The order might be just thirty meters of one design for curtains and twelve meters for a sofa. We make to measure minimum orders of as small as ten meters for the hand looms and thirty meters for the mechanical looms. (The standard minimum is 200 meters.) We can also weave the trims at the same time with the same threads, ensuring a perfect match. Thus, the client is never limited by a set production, but can be guided by his or her own needs."

The weaver begins to weave the fabric on the loom. Some designs are so complex and require so much scrutiny from the weaver that only twenty-five centimeters a day (about ten inches) can be woven. Plain silks are woven at roughly eight meters a day (100 meters would be woven on a high-speed loom).

The bobbins that hold the "weft" threads (those running across the width of the fabric) are wound on a machine built in 1860. These threads are two ply—the finest possible thread—used in the highest quality silk.

A "warping machine" prepares the warp threads (those running the length of the fabric). The number of warp threads can range from 8,000 to 34,000 at Setificio; they are wound on a long spool that will then be positioned on the loom.

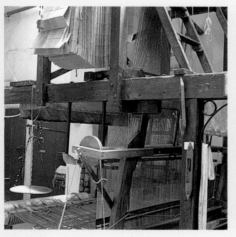

The jacquard loom is programmed with punch cards that direct the movement of the weft threads. The more complex the pattern, the greater the number of cards to direct it. A loom may hold anywhere from 1,500 to 12,000 cards. Many patterns date from the Renaissance and still carry the surname of the noble families for whom they were first designed.

Trims are created at the same time so that custom-created colors and designs are of uniform quality. Here a special loom, running on the same jacquard system used on the large looms, is set up to weave flat trim. Its warp threads are set up on a machine that was designed by Leonardo da Vinci.

VIVA IL
BAROCCO

One of the most endearing characteristics of the Italians is their seemingly limitless enthusiasm and passion for life. This same intoxicating exuberance is powerfully expressed in the art and architecture of the 1600s, the Baroque era. Artists of this period created grand and theatrical environments that celebrated the gift of human genius. As they became more conversant with the principles of perspective and the effects that could be achieved with optical illusions, artists such as the Venetian master Giambattista Tiepolo became more spirited and inventive, transposing elements from the theater, such as the proscenium arch, into backgrounds for effusive visions of heaven banked with clouds, saturated with light, and teeming with cherubs.

Today, the influence of the Baroque—and the more gentle Rococo period that followed it—continues to be felt. Just as in the seventeenth century, it does not dominate the world of design, but rather introduces a touch of lyricism and playfulness to Italian interiors and exteriors alike. The curvilinear embellishment of a wrought iron gate, the sinuous outline of a gilt mirror, or the scroll-like fruitwood base of a table are all echoes of the Baroque, adding gaiety to a room or garden that might otherwise appear too serious or stark.

ABOVE: The beauty of the Baroque is brought into this Milan home in the guise of a gilded mermaid who demurely supports a marble top across the span of her powerful wings. RIGHT: Designer Gianni Versace drew on the Baroque to inspire his collection of tableware. OPPOSITE: Gentle, lyrical curves evocative of the Rococo give a graceful presence to this bronze-framed mirror in a Venice home.

The spirit of the *Barocco* can be easily evoked through the accent pieces you choose for your interior. Good candidates would include frames, sconces, and small pedestal tables that feature curvilinear decoration.

OPPOSITE: Architect Gianni Mannocci designed and built this chair that insouciantly sports rubber pads on the seat and back.
ABOVE: Artemide's Tolomeo lamp elegantly proves that brilliant form and superb function need not be strange bedfellows.

To enhance the joy of life's little moments, consider making good design a top priority when selecting such utilitarian things as vegetable peelers, citrus juicers, nightlights — even toothbrushes.

DESIGN
WITH BRIO

In the first century B.C., the Roman architect Vitruvius composed a manual for design, *Ten Books of Architecture*, that was to set the standard for centuries to follow. In his words, the well-trained architect should be *"educated, skillful with a pencil, instructed in geometry, know much history, have followed the philosophers with attention, understand music, have some knowledge of medicine, know the opinions of the jurists, and be acquainted with astronomy and the theory of the heavens."* Clearly, such standards were so ambitious that only the best and the brightest young Romans were accepted into the ranks of these highly regarded professionals.

Two thousand years have passed since Vitruvius set his opinions to paper, but the Italians have never lost their enthusiasm for brilliant engineering and design. Like their devotion to opera, fashion, and soccer, their love of design spans all ages and levels of society. Italians are true connoisseurs of what they love; their passion is bred in them from birth, and is honed and exercised throughout their lives. The appetite for beautiful things ranges across all categories, from the watch encircling a wrist, to the telephone poised upon the desk, to the car standing at the curb.

Every object is carefully selected for three important and interdependent reasons. First, in an interior free of clutter, all objects must stand on their own merit. Second, obsolescence is not planned;

objects are expected to last a lifetime. Third, *la bellezza*—beauty—is intrinsic to the joy of life. Italians understand that if one makes choices based on these criteria, selecting objects that are crafted both for utility and delight, then their arrangement can be made with perfect confidence and great pleasure.

RIGHT: Admiring the work of Picasso, Gianni and Katarina Mannocci crafted this headboard for their bed. They also designed and handpainted the blue bedcover ornamented with hieroglyphic-like motifs. BELOW: Homework is less of a chore for Filippo Mondadori at his desk inspired by the Disney film *101 Dalmatians*. FAR RIGHT: In the Milan town house of Katherine Mondadori, a sleek polished-aluminum lamp rises from its base at an eye-catching angle.

NEVER FEEL INTIMIDATED WHEN IT COMES
TO EXPRESSING YOUR CREATIVE URGES;
THE OBJECTIVE IS TO NOURISH YOUR
SOUL, NOT TO WIN A DESIGN AWARD.
START ON A SCALE THAT FEELS COMFORT-
ABLE TO YOU—PERHAPS ANNOTATING A
SPECIAL COLLECTION OF FAMILY PHO-
TOGRAPHS IN YOUR OWN SCRIPT—AND
THEN GO WHEREVER YOUR IMAGINATION
LEADS YOU.

CREATIVITY
BEGINS AT HOME

Italian culture reached its zenith during the Renaissance, when the innovations of countless artists forever changed the course of art, architecture, and design. One of the most striking qualities of these artists was their versatility. Leonardo da Vinci, for example, was a genius whose prodigious imagination gave birth not only to paintings such as the *Mona Lisa*, but also to scores of notebooks exploring ideas for everything from bridges to flying machines. And Michelangelo, equally as energetic, turned restlessly from sculpture to painting to architecture to poetry to satisfy his creative impulses. The very term "Renaissance man" was coined to describe a person of many talents, infinite curiosity, and a passion to create.

But Italians in general have never been tempted to define their abilities too narrowly. It is this passion to create freely that gives the Italian home its distinctively individual identity. Italians, quite simply, like to make things and they like to make things that work. They admire ingenuity and revere craft. Their desire to create also reinforces the two values Italians cherish above all else: Home and Family. The hours devoted to crafts enable them to spend time together at home.

Florence resident Giovanna Baquis is accomplished at many crafts, including needlepoint and sewing. Here, she fits a tissue pattern she has just created for a cape onto her dressmaker's dummy. The cape will eventually be worn by her daughter Gisella.

BELOW: Two years ago, Giovanna Baquis created Carnevale costumes based on a deck of cards. Here are two of the players, the Queen of Spades and the Queen of Hearts.
RIGHT: The members of Alessandra Pezzati's family express their creative energy in many ways, including oil painting. Here Sandra works on her latest canvas in the afternoon light of a midsummer day.

OPPOSITE: A Milan couple celebrated their wedding by painting a Magritte-inspired trompe l'oeil on the kitchen door. The husband is a journalist for the Italian newspaper *La Repubblica*, hence the mock headline announcement MATRIMONIO LONARDI VISCONTI.

While time-honored crafts such as knitting, sewing, and needlepoint still thrive, many Italians undertake more ambitious projects to enhance their homes, such as designing and building furniture or inventing a new storage solution to hide a television or stereo. Unerring confidence in the link between their imagination and their hands inspires them to give a try to any project that strikes their fancy.

RIGHT: Giovanna Baquis works on a canvas that will be used to re-cover a footstool. BELOW: Rosanna Pezzati, Alessandra's mother, is renowned for the fantastic hats she designs each year for Carnevale. On the edge of the sofa is a collection from recent years.

ABOVE: Two views of a sleek and mobile cabinet that houses the Mannoccis' stereo. The cover is patterned after a rolltop desk and is playfully accentuated by the raspberry-and-purple side panels. BELOW: What is the logical answer to creating functional work space in a narrow kitchen? A swivel table mounted on a small spoked wheel. During the preparation of meals the lower shelf swings out into the kitchen, doubling the amount of work space. After cleanup, it tucks back against the wall.

SEEING THE
LIGHT

The Italians did not invent the candle, but they can justly lay claim to almost every other major artistic advance in lighting design. Absorbed to the point of obsession by the challenge of disseminating artificial light, they have created designs ranging from the exquisite glass-globed *cesendelli*, or hanging lamps suspended from ceilings in Renaissance Italy, to the oft-copied Tizio, a sleek and narrow flexible-armed black table lamp that has become an icon of design since its debut in 1972. Indeed, the Tizio lamp, manufactured by Artemide, sums up the ideal for controlled illumination: it offers an intelligent response to task lighting; it perfectly adjusts and adapts to its environment; and it is so impeccably designed that it earned a place in the Design Collection of the Museum of Modern Art in New York.

Another landmark development in lighting design was Italian as well. The Arco lamp from Flos was introduced in the early 1960s, when lighting design was just breaking free of the traditional mold. A floor lamp, the Arco consists of a sweeping arc of polished steel bolted to a chunk of marble at its base; the head of the lamp is a simple bowl that shields the bulb. The steel arc is so grand it can lean over a dining table, thus liberating the room from a stationary pendant or chandelier. If the table needs to be moved, the lamp moves with it or is pivoted. Standing lamps remain an indispensable compo-

FRISBI

ARCO

ICARO

TIZIO

nent of Italian interiors, in part because of the Italian preference for minimal furnishings of unassailable pedigree, and in part because they want to keep tabletops free of clutter.

The relatively recent invention of the halogen light bulb has profoundly influenced the way Italians add illumination to a room. Halogens emit a clean, bright, white light from a miniature bulb that consumes little electricity. Although ill-suited to general lighting, halogens are enormously efficient for spot lighting, creating dramatic pools of light. They can also be housed in sleek fixtures. Following the Italian preference for smooth surfaces and concealed objects, a tiny halogen light can be slid along a reed-thin track, recessed into the ceiling, or concealed in a soffit. A favored technique of architects or remodelers, in fact, is to box in a soffit over a work area or over a sink so that the source of illumination can be hidden.

FAR LEFT: Murano, Italy, has long been famous for the exquisite chandeliers made by the island's artisans. This lamp is delicately edged in red and blue and decorated with softly colored flowers.
LEFT, TOP TO BOTTOM: The Frisbi lamp was designed by Achille Castiglioni for Flos in 1977. A disk suspended from three fine steel wires diffuses the light. The arched design of Castiglioni's Arco lamp for Flos was a lighting breakthrough in 1962. The Icaro lamp was designed by Carlo Forcolini for Artemide in 1984. Perforated aluminum "wings" diffuse the light from the tube-shaped halogen bulb. The Tizio lamp, designed in 1972 by Richard Sapper for Artemide, earned a place in the Design Collection of New York's Museum of Modern Art.

FROM THE ARTISAN'S HAND

♧

A **LIGHT** FROM **VENICE**

Mariano Fortuny (1871–1949) was and is renowned for his artistry in textiles and especially for his gossamer-fine, pleated silk gowns, velvet cloaks, and Turkish-inspired cotton prints. Few of his admirers realize, however, that Fortuny was a true Renaissance man in the mold of Leonardo da Vinci; his prodigious imagination reached far beyond the narrowly circumscribed worlds of textile and dress design. Fortuny, in fact, was accomplished in many disciplines: painting, photography, architecture, engraving, stage design, and lighting. He was well versed in chemistry and physics and held the patents for a wide range of objects, from boat propellers to textile printing processes. One of his greatest inventions is so commonplace as to be taken for granted: the dimmer switch.

At the turn of the century, Fortuny focused his energies on the creation of sets for the theater. Inspired by the music and operas of composer Richard Wagner, he had begun to experiment with applying the newly invented electric light to the world of stage design. He soon realized that by manipulating the way light fell upon a painted scrim or backdrop, mood could be altered, while still retaining the basic integrity of the stage setting. This same tenet holds true of a room; its mood can be subtly or dramatically affected by light.

In retrospect it seems natural that Fortuny, master painter, engineer, and set designer, should create a series of stunning and innovative lamps that are still in production today. As he wrote in 1904: *If one lets a ray of sunlight into a darkened room, one will see a shaft of light piercing the air, but the room will not be lit up. If one then introduces a white leaf of paper in front of this shaft, the light will break up and illuminate the whole room; and yet the actual quantity of light entering still remains the same in both cases. This experiment proves that it is not the quantity, but the quality of light that makes things visible and allows the pupil of the eye to open properly.*

Built on this insight, his system for lighting stage sets consisted of collapsible domes composed of layers of opaque cloth mounted on wire structures. It also served as inspiration for a breathtaking collection of silk lamps.

Fortuny's lamps use a concave surface to subtly radiate and diffuse light. Opalescent silk is stretched over a meticulously balanced wire form, creating a dazzling silhouette. The silk is then handpainted in exotic motifs and decorated with glass beads and silk cording.

TOP: This spherically shaped lamp, the Scudo Saraceno, recalls the shields used by Ottoman warriors. BOTTOM: These elegantly spiraled Cesendello lamps, designed by Fortuny at the turn of the century, evoke the twist of Islamic turbans.

Lino Lando, founder of Venetia Studium.

Un Colpo d'Amore

Lino Lando, the owner of Venetia Studium in Venice where Fortuny lamps are reproduced, remembers well the *colpo d'amore,* or love at first sight, he experienced when he first laid eyes on Mariano Fortuny's creations.

I was seventeen years old. I walked into the Fortuny museum here in Venice, and— feeling as if an arrow had been shot directly into my heart—I was transfixed by these magnificent silk lamps. After many visits to the museum, to be near the lamps, I asked Mario, the guard there, if I could touch the lamps. I was so taken with their delicacy.

Not only did Mario say no, he startled Lando with his prediction that in ten or twenty years the lamps would disappear. Because Fortuny had insisted on using the finest, lightest silks, the aged material was so fragile it was decomposing.

Lando could not let the lamps disap- pear. Obsessed with preserving them, for years he tried to persuade the museum to permit him to make tracings of the lamps so they could be reproduced. Finally in 1981 he received permission and, working with a small team, began a series of experiments to recover the techniques Fortuny had used to create his masterpieces. The process proved far more elusive than anticipated; in fact, it took three years to refine and gave Lando a profound appreciation for the Fortuny genius. In 1984, Venetia Studium introduced its first lamps; the atelier also began to reissue the pleated silk garments and accessories for which Fortuny was so famous.

Lando often compares the process of working with the silk lamps to that of creating hand-blown glass, another noteworthy example of Venetian handi- craft. Both materials can be molded. Both are translucent. Both are extremely fragile. And both take the touch of a master artisan to realize their beauty and render their full magic.

This three-tiered silk lamp is the Scheherazade model created by Venetia Studium. It is made from pure silk, painted by hand in Turkish-Venetian motifs, and decorated with a Murano glass pearl. It hangs from beaded silk cording.

Spending an afternoon in the Venetia Studium's workshop, I got a firsthand look at the technical challenges Lando and his team had to overcome. Each lamp is entirely made by hand and, depending on the model, can take up to a week or more to complete.

The first step is to construct a metal frame. Because the frame is the support on which the lamp relies, it must be perfectly balanced. If the balance is off just a fraction, the silk will not cling properly to the frame and the lamp will not hang correctly.

The silk is saturated with water, centered, then stretched taut over the frame. It is allowed to dry.

Once dry, the silk is hand-sewn to the frame. This requires much skill as the silk must stay perfectly centered and free of wrinkles during the process.

Working with tracings of Fortuny's original designs, artists paint the silk.

The cord from which the lamp will be suspended is precisely centered on and attached to the frame.

Finally, glass beads made on the near-by island of Murano are attached to the finished lamp. (SEE RESOURCES.)

THE
LIVING
ROOM

IN A LAND WHERE a passing *come sta*—how's it going?—can easily absorb half an hour, it would be redundant to say that visiting is an important part of life. The *salotto*, the room where Italians visit, holds a key place in the house, so key, in fact, that it is hard to imagine this heart of the Italian home has not existed in its present form for centuries. Yet during the Renaissance and up until the nine-

For the living room of her Milan apartment, Marina Giusti wanted to re-create the feeling of Venice. She chose richly patterned silk damasks for the three sofas used to define the conversation area. The clean rectilinearity of the space is further defined by the shape of the coffee table.

teenth century, both the city palazzo and the country villa were designed with a decidedly unintimate *sala*, a large, all-purpose room used for dining, dancing, theatrical performances, and ceremonies. Smaller rooms, called *camere*, were reserved for quiet, intimate visits, for study, or for sleeping. Today, however, the generations gather in a living room of more moderate proportions, where, surrounded by the family's finest furnishings and possessions, they share all of life's concerns, grand and small.

PERFECTION, THY NAME IS GEOMETRY

A preference for clean lines, right angles, and perfect symmetry is quintessentially Italian. It was an Italian scholar, Vitruvius, who came up with the ingenious equation of perfect symmetry (later famously sketched by Leonardo da Vinci) based on the circle and the square formed by the human body. A compass centered at the navel, he pointed out, describes a perfect circle on which the fingers and toes of the outstretched limbs will fall. And the proportions of a perfect square are found in the height from the soles of the feet to the top of the head, by the width of the outstretched arms.

Italian living rooms might today be described as safe havens for the right

Clean, elegant lines characterize this room designed by Verdi Visconti. The long coffee table works to accentuate the sweep of the sofa.

angle. In both the selection and arrangement of furnishings, living rooms have a clean, quadrangular feel. And the determining factor in defining the rectangle or square is the choice of sofa, or, more accurately, sofas. Italians favor long, oversized sofas with a clear, distinct silhouette. In many living rooms, two sofas of equal length will be placed at right angles or directly across from each other; it is not uncommon to find three sofas positioned so that they constitute three sides of a square or rectangle.

The horizontality of the sofas is very often uninterrupted. Many arrangements omit a coffee table, or when a coffee table is present, it is placed at some distance from the sofa, as much as two feet or more. Instead, a side table may be wedged in the right angle formed by two sofas, reinforcing the impression of the overall rectangle. The introduction of chairs or an ottoman into the scheme is not common; if brought into the group, a club chair or an occasional chair is used to emphasize the crisp rectilinearity of the arrangement.

Away from the main seating group, the overall feeling of symmetry and spaciousness in the living room is maintained with the placement of just a few carefully selected furnishings.

Italians favor long sofas with a distinct silhouette. Here, three black sofas form a rectangle around the coffee table. An occasional table is wedged into the right angle formed by two sofas, while another flanks the opposite side. Note the distance between the sofas and the coffee table.
Photo by Genovese/Stylograph

To create a clean rectilinear feeling in your living room, consider the options for arranging your furniture. Can sofas be placed at right angles, or parallel to one another? Would a new coffee table help to accentuate the lines of a rectangular seating group? Do you have a square occasional table that could be placed to fill the corner formed by the two sofas? Is anything placed at an oblique angle that could be repositioned? There may be many small changes you can make that will result in the uncluttered, elegant look of an Italian interior.

BELOW: The conversation group in Katherine Mondadori's Milan town house is a picture of perfect symmetry. The sofas, covered in playfully bright primary colors, sit parallel to one another, divided by a long rectangular coffee table.

LIFE IN THE **HORIZONTAL** LANE

In the 1553 domestic inventory of the Medici family, one of the seating pieces described measured *quattro bracci*, or four arms in length. More than four hundred years later, the most popular Italian seating designs echo the long, horizontal lines of the bench belonging to the illustrious Florentine family.

The form and silhouette of today's sofas were developed in the greatest epoch

flexible metal strips were suspended that, in turn, supported three seat cushions. That sofa, called the "Bastiano," remains in production at Knoll.

Six years later, Scarpa designed the "Coronado" for another one of Italy's premier firms, B&B. With this design he inaugurated the use of a process called "cold-molded foaming," which had not previously been employed for padded

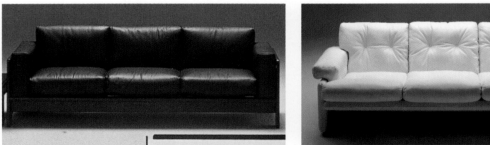

The Bastiano, by Tobia Scarpa for Knoll

The Coronado, by Tobia Scarpa for B&B

in Italian design since the Renaissance: the three decades from 1960 to 1990. In 1960, Tobia Scarpa, a designer working with Gavina (which was subsequently purchased by the American company Knoll), created a couch designed in the radical manner that came to be known as "high tech." The frame of the sofa, made of solid wood, was held together by exposed bolts from which a series of thin,

furniture. In this process, liquid polyurethane is molded within a cast into which a rigid metal frame can be sunk. Once the polyurethane foam has set and dried around the frame, it is padded, upholstered, and fitted with soft seat and back cushions.

The cushions of many Italian sofas are executed in glove-soft leather, a preference that seems logical enough for a nation enamored of luxurious car interiors and renowned the world over for its artistry in gloves, shoes, and handbags crafted of this sumptuously supple material. Leather is a most forgiving material, and perfectly suited to linear forms. It can be fitted around any frame without fear of ripping or raveling as a fiber would. In most cases, the leather used on an Italian sofa, be it burnished to a sheen or brushed

interior design became both more opulent and more oriented toward comfort, the industrial look began to be toned down. Instead, sofas were engineered with movable parts to enhance ease; arms, back, or headrest could be tilted and set in various positions. One such piece is the "Alanda," which was manufactured in 1980; it was created by the designer Paolo Piva for B&B. During the eighties the

The Diesis, by Citterio & Nava for B&B

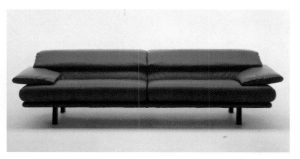

The Alanda, by Paolo Piva for B&B

soft like suede, will be marked only by bold stitching along the seams; no skirt draws the eye toward the floor, interrupting the clean lines of the silhouette and giving the sofa a heavy, earthbound look.

In the 1970s, sofas assumed an even more high-tech profile. In one example, the 1979 "Diesis" designed by Citterio and Nava for B&B, the metal frame is totally exposed. During the 1980s, as

Italians also invented the relaxed "saddlebag" arm; often crafted of leather, this arm looks like a pillow resting upon and draped over the frame.

These sofas are indispensable elements in creating the clean elegant lines that characterize Italian interiors. Arranged in groups of two or three, or even standing alone, they will continue to look fresh well into the next millennium.

WHILE ITALIAN STUCCO WALLS ARE BUILT
UPON A BRICK AND CEMENT BASE, A REAL
PLASTER FINISH CAN BE CREATED USING
GYPSUM-BOARD, OR SHEETROCK, WHICH
IS THE MOST COMMON MATERIAL USED IN
WALL CONSTRUCTION IN THE UNITED
STATES. THE PROCESS IS CALLED VENEER
PLASTER AND, AS THE NAME IMPLIES, IT
ENTAILS A THIN COAT (OR COATS) OF
PLASTER TROWELED ONTO A SPECIAL
GYPSUM-BOARD SURFACE CALLED "BLUE
BOARD," WHICH COMES IN HIGHLY
ABSORBENT PANELS. AVAILABLE
THROUGH DEALERS IN THE UNITED
STATES (SEE RESOURCES), VENEER
PLASTER OFFERS AN AUTHENTIC LOOK
FOR JUST A BIT MORE THAN A STANDARD
GYPSUM-BOARD WALL WOULD COST.

The majority of Italian walls are finished in white
or softly hued plaster. Here, the wall is gently
sponged in a rose tint, which is warmed by yellow undertones.

THE SUBTLE BEAUTY OF STUCCO WALLS

With few exceptions (notably in Venice, where walls are often papered or upholstered in richly colored, lyrically classic motifs), Italian walls display the gracefully flowing texture of handcrafted stucco or plaster. Stucco comes from the verb *stuccare*, meaning "to plaster" or "to putty." It is by far the preferred choice for walls in Italy, due to the subtle texture and richness it imparts to a room.

The recipe for stucco is simple: one-half part cement, two parts sand, and three parts lime. By varying the quality of sand introduced into the mix, the stucco can be customized to produce a range of finishes, from smooth and refined to coarse and rustic. Once the skim coat is laid down, the wall is finished in creamy white or in pale tones of peach, butter, or rose. In country homes of recent construction, the skim coat may be omitted altogether and the tint is applied directly to the concrete for a more rustic effect. (See How to Make a New Old Wall, page 51.)

Stunning tints can be achieved on stucco walls. To attain the desired tone, the artisan thoroughly mixes one or more pigments into the plain stucco before it is applied to the wall. As he spreads the stucco onto the base coat, he varies the pressure on his trowel, modulating the density of color on the wall. Or, to create a marbleized appearance, the artisan may only slightly stir the pigments in the stucco. As the stucco is spread across the surface of the wall, rich streaks of pigment appear, which, if preferred, can be minimized by blending them in a second pass with the trowel.

For an easy and informal look, stucco is typically left in its natural color and worked into the wall in a single application. It may be decorated with a stenciled border running the periphery of the room at chair rail height or higher up toward the ceiling. In Tuscany and Umbria, a trompe l'oeil baseboard is often painted around the room. About twelve inches in height, it not only creates a pleasing color accent, but also serves to camouflage the scuffs that would otherwise mar the white surface.

To re-create the beautiful color washes seen so often on the exteriors of seaside houses, a technique called *tinta a calce,* or tinted lime, that dates back to the fifteenth century, is coming back into vogue. The *tinta,* a runny blend of sand, lime, cement, and pigments such as ochre, raspberry, or watery teal, is casually brushed over the white undercoat. The effect is warm, subtle, and deliciously evocative of the sunny Mediterranean.

Architect Riccardo Caracciolo selected a wrought iron stair rail mounted with playful hand-shaped brass hardware for the classic white stucco walls of his farmhouse in Umbria.

HOW TO MAKE A **NEW OLD** WALL

Architect Riccardo Caracciolo, who specializes in the restoration of classic *case coloniche,* or farmhouses, in his native Umbria, took me through several renovations he was directing in the hilltop towns near Todi and Orvieto. In two or three homes the existing space was being repartitioned, which gave me a chance to see up close the Italian process of constructing a wall.

Approximately every thirty inches, a vertical strip of cement about three inches wide and two inches deep is troweled directly to the wall. These strips will serve as a guide for the artisans when they start to apply cement to the entire surface of the wall. At this point conduits and pipes are installed for telephone, electricity, plumbing, and cable television. The plumbers and electricians follow the guide of the cement strips, being careful not to exceed the final surface thickness.

Cement is applied to the wall to fill in the gaps between all the strips and to cover the conduits. A level is guided along the surface of the strips to smooth the cement to a constant thickness.

Exposed edges are made square with two-by-fours clamped in position on the damp cement. When the cement has set and dried, the clamps and two-by-fours are removed and the surface of the wall is prepared for stucco or paint.

To prepare the surface to receive its base coat and finish coats of stucco, the wall is washed to remove any accumulated dust or dirt and to provide the damp surface to which the stucco must adhere. Once the white undercoat has been fully applied, the final pigmented coat will be mixed. For a uniform color, it will be mixed to a thick consistency and worked into the base coat. If just a color wash is desired, a thinner mixture will be brushed onto the wall. For a rough, more rustic look, no stucco is applied. Two coats of paint are instead brushed directly onto the raw cement.

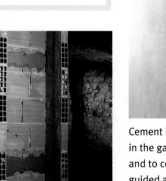

The core of the wall is created using terra-cotta bricks, three inches in width. The bricks are honeycombed, which gives them superior strength without adding weight.

DECORATING THE WALLS

"I suppose the difference between working on a Sheetrock wall and working on a plaster wall is analogous to the difference an artist would feel between painting on paper and painting on canvas," says Florence-born architect Alessandro Corsini. "Certainly, we can do an eight-color stencil process on the Sheetrock and give it some depth, but it can never equal the enormously rich colorations that can be achieved on plaster."

Corsini, who now works almost exclusively in the United States, likes to impart a warmth to the walls he decorates. When working with paints, regardless of the final color desired, he begins with a base coat of yellow. It makes the warm colors even warmer, and prevents the blues and greens from becoming too cold. After the final coat is applied and has dried, the walls are lightly sanded so that bits of the warm yellow undercoat can be pulled through. Finally, the surface is glazed, which renders all the colors deeper and richer. The motifs and colors are often inspired from the works of Renaissance painters. Studying the masterpieces of Botticelli or Ghirlandaio, for example, Corsini will focus on the decorative border of a sleeve or a particular shade of burgundy depicted in a mural. "These inspirations are so readily available to all of us," he says. "I often wonder how the artists would react if they were to learn that four hundred years later, their work is still so appealing."

When working with stucco walls, one of the most beautiful decorating options features a process called *stucco lustro.* In this process, several layers of a thin blend of lime, pigment, and water are brushed onto the wall surface; the wall is then finished with a polish of beeswax, which gives a rich, deep luster to the work. As an additional step, where budgets allow, the stucco may be decoratively painted. Corsini's cousin Nencia Corsini, an artist trained in her native Italy, sketches lyrical patterns on top of the finished stucco, then paints them in gold, resulting in a warm and sumptuous look (see page 54).

Although artisanally applied stucco remains a relatively complicated process, in recent years some products have come onto the market to make it a bit easier. Ready-made primer, for example, is a sort of sandpaperlike product that is rolled onto the wall and then covered with one or two layers of stucco. While this doesn't make the process quick and easy, it does save a significant amount of time and effort

OPPOSITE: Architect Alessandro Corsini and his cousin Nencia Corsini used an eight-color stencil process on the plaster walls of this New York City apartment. After Nencia finished applying the paint, she washed the wall with a sepia-colored stain and applied beeswax to deepen the luster. *Photo by I. Terestchenko*

over the traditional methods.

Trompe l'oeil is also used as a decorative technique on Italian walls. Although the name is French, the technique actually has its origins in Italy. Once painters of the Renaissance had discovered the principles of perspective, they began to create dazzling renditions of architectural elements, both in their easel paintings and in frescoes. These frescoes so "fooled the eye" that noblemen who visited from France persuaded armies of these talented artisans to emigrate and decorate the walls of their châteaux.

Trompe l'oeil was an illusionary technique that enhanced the feeling of splendor and luxury for a fraction of the cost of applied architectural elements. Visually arresting features such as columns, pilasters, cornices, and pediments, copied from Greek or Roman prototypes, were painted on the walls. Coupled with the Italian love of theatricality, these faux architectural surrounds imparted a sense of drama and grandeur to a room.

ABOVE: The trompe l'oeil technique is applied to enhance a door. LEFT: A stenciled wall. BELOW: Two doorways are visually united by a trompe l'oeil design. OPPOSITE: A narrow corridor springs to life with a trompe l'oeil painted by Nencia Corsini. The wainscoting and vertical stripes give architectural definition to the space.

OVERLEAF, LEFT: Pigmented stucco can be even further enhanced by hand-painted decoration. Nencia Corsini sketched curvilinear motifs on top of finished stucco and then applied gold paint. *Photo by I. Terestchenko* RIGHT: Classical architectural elements are often the subject of trompe l'oeil paintings. Here in the dining room of Fiamma di San Giuliano Ferragamo, the effect is enchanting.

THE
LIVING
ROOM

57

For a less expensive substitute for terrazzo, a simulated vinyl "terrazzo" containing marble chips is now available in many different colorations. This vinyl flooring product has the advantages of easy installation and a relatively moderate cost of less than $8.00 per square foot; it is also softer and warmer underfoot than real terrazzo. It is particularly well suited to entrance halls, kitchens, and laundry rooms. (See Resources.)

THE **FLOOR,**
REVEALED

Italian floors are impressive, not only for the extravagance of their materials, but also for the complex patterns they exhibit. Historically, many of these patterns took their inspiration from the dazzling motifs found on oriental rugs that entered Italy through the port of Venice. Renaissance craftsmen worked with multicolored marbles or tiles to create starbursts, latticeworks, and other impressive designs. Sophisticated engineering techniques allowed builders to support floors of considerable weight, and so materials such as marble, earthenware tiles, and stone could be installed not only on the *piano nobile*, or first floor, but also on the floors above.

Tile, in fact, is the most popular medium for covering a floor, and from Rome northward through Tuscany, terra-cotta tiles dominate. These fired-clay tiles can be molded and sliced into a wide range of shapes, including squares, rectangles, diamonds, hexagons, octagons, or even circles. The geometric flexibility allows tile to be installed in an array of patterns. Rectangular tiles, for example, can be laid in a herringbone configuration; when the tiles are very narrow, the effect can be quite dramatic. Square tiles, or multiples of four or eight squares, can be surrounded, or framed, with rectangles; the entire floor surface can also be bordered with a running series of same-size rectangles. When squares and rectangles are combined, crosses or lattice effects can be created.

The surface of the terra-cotta floors can be grouted and polished, left roughly textured, or sealed to resist moisture and stains in high-traffic areas.

South of Rome, ceramic is the material of choice for floor tiles. Italians are famed for their brightly colored glazed ceramic tiles, and especially for large tiles that are over twelve inches square. The glaze is typically a very high gloss; such tiles are laid as close together as possible, with little or no grout, to create a smooth, unbroken plane.

Because marble is a readily available natural resource, it is widely used in the Italian home whenever a more luxurious and refined finish is desired. In many city houses and apartments, marble will be used in the entry hall, set in a pattern such as a starburst or lattice. The relatively limited space keeps the purchase price of the marble within reach yet allows an elegant tone to be set from the moment one enters the home. Terrazzo—a mix of marble chips, crushed stone, and stucco—is a less costly alternative to marble. The floor is installed in several thin layers; as each layer is poured, it is compacted. Once the desired thickness and textural effect have been achieved, the floor is allowed to

LEFT: The entryway of the Pezzati home in Florence is classically elegant with its marble floor and trompe l'oeil marble columns. The marble is always maintained to a rich shine. FAR LEFT: A striking configuration of terra-cotta tiles gives a distinct personality to the entryway of this Umbrian home. Note how effectively the circular tile in the center of the floor works to provide a focal point to the design.

harden and set, then it is polished to a fine sheen.

Filling out the range of stone flooring materials is slate, which is often used in contemporary homes decorated with a nod toward Milan's high-tech look, along with granite, limestone, and flagstone. If a hard, stonelike surface is desired, but budgets are limited, cement may be pigmented to simulate the effect of traditional *pavimenti*.

Wooden floors are treated like those set in tile; in other words, instead of laying strips or planks, the Italians concentrate on the effects that can be achieved with parquet. Herringbone, basketweave, and framed squares are the most common patterns to be found. Many wooden floors incorporate several species of hardwood in one design; oak and beech are two standards. Because wooden floors are so prized, they are meticulously maintained, always polished and buffed to a shine.

With so much effort and expense invested in the floor, it is little wonder that wall-to-wall carpeting is rarely found in Italy. Instead, if a floor is to be covered at all, it will be with a collection of small oriental rugs or kilims, and then only to define seating areas. Sisal is gaining in popularity as a low-cost alternative to woven rugs. In the few instances where carpet is used, it is the tight, Berber-style, neutral-toned type common to commercial installations.

The warmth of cherry creates a magnificent floor. Note how the sparse furnishings of the room allow one to fully appreciate the richness of the wood.
Photo by Sancassani/Stylograph

CARING FOR YOUR FLOOR

Italians invest as much energy into the maintenance of their floors as they do in selecting and installing them. Following are the traditional methods of care for each type of floor.

TERRA-COTTA: For four or five months after the installation, mop the floor daily with a rag soaked in raw linseed oil. When dry, polish lightly with a wool rag. When the tiles have achieved the rich color desired, have them machine polished with a good floor wax. Thereafter, the floor should be swept on a daily basis. Clean as you would marble and tile.

MARBLE AND TILE: On a weekly basis the floor should be damp mopped with a diluted mixture of water and detergent. When dry, rag mop with a small amount of floor wax. Finish with a dry wool rag to eliminate any streaks. For a more brilliant shine, add a few drops of alcohol to the floor wax, brush very lightly on the floor, let dry well, and then buff with a wool rag.

WOOD: Sweep floors as needed. Once a week, mop with a barely damp rag mop. When the floor looks dull, apply a good-quality floor wax and buff. Use spray wax for small spots, wiping clean with a wool rag.

TOP: This starburst pattern painted on the wooden floor of a Milan apartment shows how effectively trompe l'oeil can be used to create the appearance of marquetry. BOTTOM: The blue-gray slate tiles on this living-room floor provide an easy-care surface and complement the contemporary furnishings.

CLEAN, ELEGANT
WINDOWS

Echoing the manner in which they dress themselves, Italians treat their windows with quiet elegance and restraint. Nearly every window in Italy is, in fact, dressed in one of two ways: a transverse rod crafted of wrought iron or occasionally wood, with ball-shaped finials, is mounted above the window with pleated curtains suspended from it on rings; or a pelmet is installed and draperies descend from behind it. In both cases, the curtains or draperies drop to within one inch of the floor. It is very rare to see draperies pooling on the floor in Italy.

Fabrics preferred for window treatments in a contemporary interior are lightweight cotton or linen, and, occasionally, silk. Because the fabric serves to provide privacy without sacrificing light, it is generally light in color, typically white or cream, or a pale pastel. If privacy is not an issue, the windows will often be left undressed. In traditionally decorated homes, the fabrics used will be more richly colored and textured; jacquards and damasks in cotton or silk are popular choices. Both the pelmet and the draperies will be trimmed in a refined, sophisticated style. For example, a simple flat braid or gimp made from silk can be applied to the border and tassels can accent the tiebacks.

LEFT: Italian windows are dressed with quiet elegance. In the Florence home of the Antinori family, a formal style of drapery handsomely trimmed with a flat braid has been selected for the windows leading out to the garden.

RIGHT: Long red draperies, accented with tiebacks of blue silk cording, fall to just within an inch of the floor. The owner had the valence made from lacquered fabric, which is maintained simply by occasional vacuuming. BELOW: The simple white linen draperies in this re-stored farmhouse are typical of the style se-lected by most Italians. Here the transverse rod and rings are made of wood, but often they are wrought iron.

WHEN SELECTING FABRIC FOR WIN-DOW TREATMENTS, LOOK FOR SOLIDS OR SUBTLE PATTERNS OF THE HIGHEST QUALITY CLOTH YOUR BUD-GET PERMITS. THE OBJECTIVE IS TO GIVE THE WINDOW AN ELEGANT, FIN-ISHED LOOK—NOT TO MAKE IT THE FOCAL POINT OF THE ROOM.

Any discussion of the Italian window cannot fail to mention the shutter, which blocks early morning light in the bedroom and prevents the midday heat from entering the home. Every window in Italy is equipped with a shutter, although the type of shutter varies by region or type of dwelling. In Milan and in contemporary homes throughout the century, a flexible, roll-up shutter is favored. Housed in a box mounted above the window or concealed within the wall, the shutter is guided by a flat-ribboned cord-and-pulley system.

The traditional version of the shutter is slatted and hinged midway down the shutter; the hinge allows the lower half of the shutter to tilt outward. When braced, the tilted shutter effectively blocks light and heat, lets in air, and in cities allows a view of the street below. Some country houses replace the slatted shutter with a paneled one; this type of shutter is favored when a house—such as a vacation getaway in the mountains or by the sea—is to be shut for any length of time.

ABOVE: This solid wooden shutter opening to the inside is typical of the farmhouses in Umbria. The soft blue-green color selected has been used to dramatic effect against the white stucco walls.
LEFT: When privacy and light are not issues, as in the living room of this seaside home, windows are generally left uncovered. Note how beautifully the arch of the window frames the arches of the terrace.

THE ART OF **DISPLAY**

Considering the Italian predisposition toward clean, uncluttered environments, it is only logical that anything they collect will be displayed in such a way that each object will command, and receive, undivided attention. On the mantel, for example, it is very common to find two or three objects of similar scale grouped together with nothing else to distract from the arrangement. While these objects may be mismatched or eclectic, each will perfectly represent its genre: a ceramic signed by the artisan; a sandblasted vase from Murano, the Venetian center of glassmaking; a handturned wooden candelabrum discovered in an antiques shop. High quality is not synonymous with high cost, however. Italians pride themselves on their sharp eye and on a shrewd sense of bargaining. And with the relative abundance of skilled craftsmen, having a favorite piece reproduced is always a possibility.

Because Italians tend to be quite sociable, one type of display found in nearly every living room is a large tray for aperi-

tifs. Crystal tumblers and stemware, a selection of liquors, and other accoutrements for the bar such as an ice bucket, tongs, and martini shaker might be grouped upon an heirloom sterling silver tray. The tray is typically displayed on a console, an occasional table, or a shelf of a wall unit. The glasses, bottles, and tray shimmer alluringly by both sunlight and candlelight, but maintaining these spotless displays is not for the weakhearted. In fact, they serve as a sort of silent testimony to the impeccable standards of housekeeping maintained in Italian homes.

In the display of art, Italians again focus on clarity. Generally one single large painting will be hung on a wall, completely surrounded by white space. When several pieces are grouped together, the visual emphasis is often on the interplay between similar renditions of the same subject matter.

ABOVE: Note the clean symmetry of this display. A strong, single image dominates the oil painting centered above the credenza. Four Chinese porcelain plates are displayed with two oval platters placed on either side of the round plates. Identical table lamps are placed on each side, and three pieces of silver are arranged in the center.
RIGHT: A silver tray bearing an assortment of fine crystal glistens in the afternoon sun. Most Italian families will create this type of display in the living room, one that is as practical for serving guests as it is handsome.

RIGHT: Three stunning red pieces made in Murano command attention in the entryway of this Venice home. Note how compelling the display is, unencumbered by other objects or colorings.

TO CREATE AN ITALIAN FEELING IN YOUR DISPLAYS, MAKE YOUR FOCUS SIMPLICITY. FOR EXAMPLE, REMOVE EVERYTHING FROM THE FIREPLACE MANTEL EXCEPT FOR JUST ONE OR TWO WELL-SCALED OBJECTS THAT YOU PARTICULARLY LIKE. SIMILARLY, CONSIDER PLACING ONE LARGE COLORED GLASS VASE ALONG A LEDGE OR SHELF, OR TWO TO THREE OBJECTS OF A SINGLE COLOR ON A SMALL OCCASIONAL TABLE.

YOU CAN **ALWAYS**
GO **HOME** AGAIN

The family, and by extension the family home, are the unquestioned pillars of Italian society. In Italy, though, *family* holds a deeper meaning than the *nuclear family*, and *home* signifies more than the house in which the family dwells. Beyond a strong attachment to the place where they reside, most Italians are passionately attached to *the* Home, a property associated with the family as a whole. This homestead is the magnet that draws everyone together, the place where they come to recharge their spirits and to find solace in one another's company, in good

The DeCamilli family currently resides in America, but travels often to father Pietro's Lombardy homestead to provide the children with a strong connection to their heritage.

times and bad. "Even though I must remain in America to do research in my field," says Dr. Pietro DeCamilli, a neurobiologist at Yale University, "a part of my heart always rests in our family home in Lombardy. We travel back at least twice a year because I want my children

to know that home, to understand why I love it so."

The very idea of the Home inspires an awe-filled respect. "Our family home in Siena has existed since the thirteenth century," says Alessandro Falassi, professor of anthropology at the Università Per Stranieri in Siena. "It is the thread that connects all the generations. In fact, sometimes I feel very ephemeral compared to the house. Someday I will pass on . . . but the house will always remain."

The home is understood to be an integral part of the cycle of life, and is admired for the harmony it maintains with the landscape that embraces it, and with nature. "This house has been in our family for 700 years," says Laudomia Pucci, president of Emilio Pucci, SpA, the Florence-based fashion concern founded by her father. "You can see that it was built in a very clever way to maximize space and light. The walls are very thick, which muffles the winter cold and helps to keep the heat out in summer. The windows bring in just the right amount of light, so the house works with the seasons. When we feel the sun creeping in too much in the summer, we just temper it by slanting the shutters a bit."

The colors of the home, too, are in concert with those in nature. "Look around you," counsels Falassi, pointing to the houses dotting the hillsides around Siena. "What colors do you see: terra-cotta brick; creamy beige stone; charcoal gray marble on the cathedral. These are the colors of the earth—and these are the colors we are comfortable using. The secret of the Renaissance was to be in tune with nature, to leave your mark on nature without ever violating it." And, in fact, all over Italy, the materials in the homes reflect the mood of the landscapes in which they are situated, from the blues and sandy colors of the seaside, to the clay and wheat tones of Umbria and Tuscany, to the soft pinks of the Venetian sunsets.

The profound connection to the homestead includes the extended family that it shelters. "We make quite an effort to bring all the members of the family together—particularly around the holi-days," says Marina Giusti del Giardino, public relations director for the aperitif and spirits firm of Martini and Rossi. "Even if it makes everyone a little frantic, the effort is worth it. Getting together creates such a good feeling." Her daugh-ter Gaia elaborates. "When I'm around

my family, I feel whole, secure," she says. "The feeling of family is fundamental to us; we always know where we belong."

That sense of belonging, Giusti explains, depends upon developing and maintaining strong ties between genera-tions, and especially between children and their grandparents. "My children," she says, "love to visit their grandmother. How could we live without her stories! She holds our history and wants to share it with us."

No one pretends family relationships in Italy are free of trying moments, but the connection between parent and child, no matter what happens, is extremely important to both. This is most evident when hearing the laments about changes brought on by "modern life." "It's not the way it used to be," sighs Tia DiVen-centis, director of Palazzo Martini, the exhibition and event center in Milan owned by Martini and Rossi. "I am a

Brother and sister Alessandro and Laudomia Pucci pose for a portrait on the terrace of the family home in Florence, where they have lived since childhood. Italian families rarely sell their homestead, and indeed the Pucci family has occupied this house for 700 years.

Italian families put a high priority on spending time together, often fleeing city apartments on weekends and school vacations to relax in the countryside. ABOVE: The Mondadori family—Leonardo, Francesco, Katherine, Filippo, and Martina gather in Capri. RIGHT: Filippo plays with the family dog.

career woman with young children, so I don't have as much contact with my own mother as I would have had in another era—and that she had with hers." Sympathetically, I ask how often she talks with her mother. "Well, never more than . . . ," DiVencentis pauses to think carefully. "Never more than once a day." Seeing my surprise and realizing that in the context of American life this might, in fact, be considered a very close mother-and-daughter relationship, she quickly adds, "But I don't actually *see* her." To an Italian, daily contact is not an exception but the rule.

The pleasure of family is not built upon an expectation of any one member doing anything in particular; it relies simply on the pleasure of being near one another. As Fiamma di San Giuliano Ferragamo, vice president of the

Florentine manufacturer of fine footwear and fashion of the same name, notes, "It is always such a joy to be together. Many Sunday afternoons, when my children were growing up, were spent in the library, everyone occupied with their own activity, reading, writing letters, perhaps listening to music. We weren't necessarily entertaining each other; we just enjoyed the feeling of being together as a family in our home."

Maintaining that closeness is a significant factor in making life choices. Italians prefer to stay close to their home town, with easy access to family and friends. If taking an attractive job necessitates a move away from home, the decision-making process will be traumatic. It is one thing to travel—but quite another to leave home. "I know there are places where it might be easier for me to advance in my profession," says Carlo di Perotti, a young photographer, "but my roots are here, my life is here. I can't find this anywhere else." Winemaker Francesco Giuntini echoes di Perotti's sentiments. "The Giuntini family has been here at Selvapiana for five generations," he says. "My grandfather's grandfather began running the property in 1827, and I took it over forty years ago. Although we have faced difficult situations many times, when Selvapiana has been a source of great suffering, I feel extremely privileged to live in this beautiful countryside. I could never imagine moving away."

In Italy one thing never changes— the heart is where the Home is.

THE
BEDROOM

"THE BEDROOM IS FOR sleeping, not for strolling, dining, or dancing," admonishes one character to an apparently capricious friend in a story written by Anton Francesco Doni in Venice more than 400 years ago. The sentiment still applies. Like the rest of the Italian house, the bedroom is furnished with just a few finely made pieces: an impeccably crafted bed dressed in beautiful linens and flanked by a pair of small nightstands, an armoire, and perhaps a chair comprise the standard inventory. One enjoys not only the luxury of space but also the relaxing effect of an uncluttered room.

A beautifully crafted wrought iron bed, embellished with handpainted decorations, is the centerpiece of this bedroom in Porto Ercole. Wrought iron is a popular material for beds in Italy.

The floor and walls in the Italian bedroom create an ambience that perfectly harmonizes with its carefully selected furnishings. Floors, typically sheathed in warm woods or rosy terra-cotta, are often uncovered, accented only with small rugs on one or both sides of the bed. In the few instances when the bedroom floor is covered, it is with a flat, low-pile carpet that elegantly underscores the clean, understated lines of the room. Walls, generally painted in off-white or soft colors, are never crowded with pictures, but instead display just a few pieces with special meaning to the room's occupants. The objective is to maintain the bedroom as a private, peaceful retreat.

THE **BED**

In fifteenth-century Italy the equivalent of having a Maserati in the driveway was to have a *padiglione* in the bedroom. This was a cone- or dome-shaped crown suspended over the bed and ornately draped with rich velvets and brocades. The higher the standing of the owner in the

OPPOSITE: Italian baldachins are more often crafted from wrought iron than from wood. In designing this bed, Architect Riccardo Caracciolo opted for clean, light lines and just a simple canopy of white linen. Note the bedside tables that were designed to complement the bed and preserve its simple, elegant lines. LEFT: Over nearly every bed in Italy a representation of the Virgin Mary, or some religious symbol, crowned by a small olive branch protects the sleeper. In Marina Giusti's Milan apartment, a beautiful painting of the Virgin and Child hangs above the head of the wrought iron baldachin.

community, the more elaborate the confection enveloping the bed.

Today, while not quite retaining the high status of its Renaissance forebear, the bed is still held in great esteem. In traditionally decorated homes, the *letto matrimoniale*, or matrimonial bed, is most often framed with a substantial headboard and footboard of beautifully worked wood, wrought iron, or fine upholstery. Occasionally a bolster will run along the front of the headboard, against which a pair of pillows will rest.

The *baldacchino*, or canopy bed, is still popular today in both contemporary and traditional decors. But unlike the sinuous silhouettes of its French counterpart, the Italian canopy bed is noteworthy for its exceptionally clean rectangular lines. Its lineage can be traced to the suspended *cortinaggio*, a form of curtaining used on four-poster beds dating from the sixteenth century. Fabric was suspended from rings encircling a rectangular frame; these hangings could then be easily pulled into position without leaving the bed and the fabric would stay as adjusted. Sometimes the rectangular frame was suspended from the ceiling, although usually the rods could simply be inserted between the bedposts.

Today the posts and frame of the *baldacchino* are most likely to be made in wrought iron, which accentuates its rectilinearity. The *baldacchino* may be unadorned, it may be covered only across the top, or it may be draped on all four sides with a lightweight material, which is then gathered and tied to the posts. In every instance, the effect is pleasingly light and refined.

The bed has not emerged untouched by the design revolution of the past three decades. Taking their cue from beds of 500 years ago, which often featured built-in benches and storage, Italian design firms such as Cassina, Flou, and Molteni have created sleek, innovative bed systems that combine headboard, bed, and nightstands in one smooth-surfaced unit.

Some beds in Italy clearly reflect the influence of other European countries. One such influence is from Scandinavia. Down comforters simply draped over a good-quality mattress and frame and topped by two standard pillows can be seen in many contemporary interiors, while a Spanish influence exists in the elaborately carved and turned four-poster beds found in many traditional interiors of Italy's southern regions.

OPPOSITE, CENTER: The elaborately turned and carved posts of this bed reflect the Spanish influences that can often be seen in southern Italy. BELOW: A crisply tailored bed with upholstered platform and headboard is majestically crowned by a framed *stemma*, or family crest. Note the bedcover does not fall to the floor and the simple night table contains just a few decorative elements.

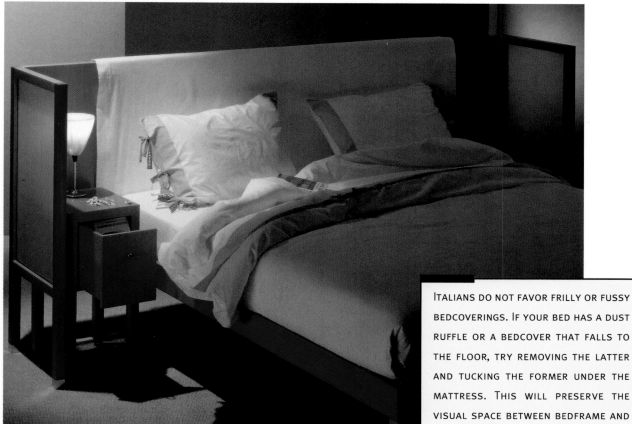

ITALIANS DO NOT FAVOR FRILLY OR FUSSY BEDCOVERINGS. IF YOUR BED HAS A DUST RUFFLE OR A BEDCOVER THAT FALLS TO THE FLOOR, TRY REMOVING THE LATTER AND TUCKING THE FORMER UNDER THE MATTRESS. THIS WILL PRESERVE THE VISUAL SPACE BETWEEN BEDFRAME AND FLOOR, GIVING YOUR ROOM A CLEANER, MORE ITALIAN LOOK.

Modern Italian design firms are producing sleek and innovative beds and bed systems. ABOVE: Cassina's Soeur Marie, designed by Philippe Starck, evokes the feeling of a screen with the design of its headboard. The same clean, rectilinear lines of the bed platform and headboard are reflected in the small night table, which tucks in between the opaque glass panel and the bed. LEFT: Flou's Meridiana bed draws its inspiration from classical eighteenth-century French models but updates the look with a smartly upholstered headboard that flows seamlessly into the frame.

SUMPTUOUS
LINENS

Traditionally, the Italian bride was to come to her marriage with *dodici di tutto*—twelve of everything. In other words, her trousseau was to include the number of fine linens needed to keep the wedding bed fresh through the cold winter months, when doing the laundry was often a difficult, if not impossible, task. The bride and the women in her family spent many hours embroidering beautiful bedding that was expected to last the lifetime of the couple, if not beyond.

Although most Italians can no longer afford a dozen sets of fine linens, they still maintain an "investment mentality" when it comes to buying and caring for their bed linens. Dr. Vittorio Mosca is president of the Milan-based Frette, a firm synonymous with fine bed and table linens. He explains, "It is like buying a Ferrari, which is neither low-cost nor maintenance-free. You accept the conditions because you believe that the quality of the product, and, by extension, your experience, is worth it."

A quality sheet is distinguished by a high thread count, which is the number of threads woven per square inch. A count of 300 will result in a very durable sheet with a marvelously silky feeling next to the skin. Optimally, the thread is a pure linen from Belgium or Northern Ireland. Known in the trade as "the noble fiber," linen exhibits qualities of both remarkable softness and exceptional strength. It has a quality of freshness that

keeps the body from overheating, making it particularly enjoyable during Italy's warm-weather months. Indeed, Italians swear that linen has a salutary effect on the body and gives a better night's sleep—an assertion difficult to prove scientifically but perhaps linked to the knowledge that the sheets will last a generation or two!

Next in quality to pure linen is 100 percent long-fiber Egyptian cotton. When woven to a 250 thread count or higher, Egyptian cotton makes a fine-quality sheet, which will grow softer with age. If properly cared for, a sheet of Egyptian cotton will have a life span of up to fifteen or twenty years. Because linen lasts longer (up to twenty-five years or more) but cotton is softer, some sheet manufacturers blend the two. Particularly prized in the Italian home are sheets or coverlets embellished with embroidery, lace, or cutwork, or made of damasked cotton, such as those produced by the Italian firms of Frette and Pratesi.

Italians maintain an investment approach toward bed linens: they buy the best they can afford, give them proper care, and thus can enjoy them for a generation or more. Here, the pillow shams and sheets are classic white damask edged in lace. The square pillow and bedcover are quilted satin-weave cotton. (SEE RESOURCES.)

Fine linens are an investment worth protecting with proper laundering and storage. Consider using the time-honored methods of Italian homekeepers. Sheets are washed and then ironed while still slightly damp. (If your machine will clean sheets satisfactorily with warm water, it is better to avoid exposing the fibers to the rigors of the "hot" setting.) Next they are neatly folded; sometimes individual sets of bed linens will be tied with ribbons and stored in an armoire for linens. If they will not be used for long periods of time, the stacks of linen are covered with acid-free tissue.

RIGHT: A classic look is accomplished by using gold damask with cutwork decoration on sheets and pillow shams. BELOW: This bed is dressed in sheets and a bedcover recalling colorful Provençal prints. (SEE RESOURCES.)

IF YOU HAVE THE SPACE IN YOUR HOME FOR A *GUARDAROBA,* OR LAUNDRY ROOM, CONSIDER INSTALLING SOME OF THE AMENITIES FOUND IN MANY ITALIAN HOMES. FIRST AND MOST IMPORTANTLY, SET UP A RECTANGULAR TABLE (FORTY-EIGHT BY THIRTY INCHES MINIMUM) THAT CAN DOUBLE, WHEN PROTECTED BY A THERMAL PAD, AS A SURFACE FOR IRONING SHEETS AND OTHER LARGE PIECES AS WELL AS FOR FOLDING THEM. IDEALLY, THIS TABLE SHOULD CONTAIN STORAGE SHELVES BELOW IT FOR THE SUPPLIES REQUIRED FOR PRESSING. CONSIDER, TOO, CONSTRUCTING A FLOOR-TO-CEILING LINEN CLOSET WITH SHELVES DEEP ENOUGH—AT LEAST TWENTY-FOUR INCHES—TO COMFORTABLY HOLD FOLDED LINENS. ALSO CONVENIENT IS A FREESTANDING RACK (SIMILAR TO THE DISPLAY RACKS FOUND IN CLOTHING STORES) FOR HANGING GARMENTS JUST OUT OF THE DRYER OR AS SOON AS THEY ARE PRESSED.

BELOW: A well-organized *armadio della biancheria*—an armoire for linens—holds towels and bedding for the master bedroom of this home in Orvieto. Note the list entitled *camera padronale,* or master bedroom, which specifies which items should be kept on the shelves and in what order they should be arranged.

A **BEDROOM**
BEN SISTEMATO

The secret to keeping the bedroom *ben sistemato*—well organized and clutter free—lies in the armoires and wall systems favored in Italian homes. The ideal wall system runs from floor to ceiling and the entire span of an unbroken interior wall. It includes cubbies, drawers, shelves, plus single- and double-bar hanging compartments. Everything is, of course, *tutto nascosto*, hidden behind doors. Although floor space may be sacrificed to the system's requisite twenty-four-inch depth, the gain in usable storage allows the remaining square footage to stay clean and feel peacefully spacious.

Wall systems can be very elaborate and include such luxuries as pocket doors that glide into the unit to provide clear access to all the shelves, sliding racks for shoes, cedar-lined compartments, and dressing mirrors. Or they may be simple, made from sturdy laminated particleboard with only a few necessary shelves and hanging compartments. Either way, they obviate the need for additional furnishings.

To maintain the peaceful tone, of the bedroom, take care not to clutter the night table or dresser. Consider only a bedside clock, a lamp, perhaps a book—plus, by Italian tradition, a photograph of one's spouse.

Most Italian bedrooms are equipped with a wall system or an armoire that offers considerable storage capacity and obviates the need for many additional furnishings. The system here is produced by Molteni & C, as are the bed and night tables.

Architect Riccardo Caracciolo transformed this shallow closet in the master bedroom of his Todi home into an armoire. The rounded crown was created to echo the arched wall above the bed shown on page 74.

A CLOSET CAN BE TRANSFORMED INTO A MODIFIED ARMOIRE, PRO-VIDING ADDITIONAL STORAGE SPACE AS WELL AS VISUAL INTEREST. IF THE CLOSET IS LESS THAN THIRTY INCHES WIDE, YOU WILL WANT TO MAKE THE FINISHED DIMENSIONS OF THE ARMOIRE EXTEND BEYOND THE EXISTING WIDTH OF THE CLOSET. REMOVE THE CLOSET DOOR AND CONSTRUCT A FRAME AROUND THE OPENING, EXTEND-ING INTO THE ROOM EIGHTEEN INCHES, OR MORE IF SPACE ALLOWS. USE THE FINEST TYPE OF WOOD YOUR BUDGET ALLOWS, AND CONSIDER ELEMENTS LIKE AN ARCHED TOP OR THE ADDITION OF A CORNICE. CONSTRUCT DOORS AND ATTACH TO THE FRAME WITH HINGES. IF THE WIDTH EXCEEDS THAT OF THE CLOSET, CON-SIDER OUTFITTING THE SHALLOW SPACE WITH SHELVES AND/OR HOOKS FOR BELTS, SCARVES, JEWELRY, AND OTHER SMALL ITEMS.

ABOVE: Marble is a typical choice for the sink surround in Italy, being both beautiful and practical for an area that will be exposed to water.

RIGHT: The late afternoon sun sweeps across ceramic tiles of the tub in this restored farmhouse. Many Italian homes do not have showers, featuring instead a handheld spray like the one at right. Note the trompe l'oeil baseboard painted on the wall.

THE **BATH**

Private bathing rooms were included in grander Italian homes from as early as the fifteenth century. Without the benefit of electricity or central water supplies, clever hydraulic engineers and highly specialized craftsmen worked in clay, metal, and glass to devise jointed piping systems, woodstove boilers for heating water, taps, and tile and marble fixtures. Linen cloths were sometimes draped inside the tub so that one's skin would not come in contact with hard marble. Intricate mosaics might be made in the shape of fish so that their "scales" would shimmer when covered with water. The bathroom was indeed a sign of status.

Today, the bathroom continues to profit from tile and marble. As practical as it is beautiful, tile is used on most or all of the wall surface. Myriad patterns are created using the vast range of handpainted tile manufactured in Italy. Depending on the look desired, decorated tiles are interspersed with white or solid color tiles. If the budget permits, marble, easily quarried in Italy, is a favorite material for countertops as well as for the bath and shower. Many homes in Italy contain just a bath with a handheld spray; a shower is found only in newer or renovated homes.

Like the rest of the home, the bathroom is not burdened by clutter. Cabinets and closets keep supplies close at hand but never out in view. A minimum of toiletries are displayed on the countertop: soap, fragrance, and perhaps some lavender or a nosegay of fresh flowers.

THE
DINING
ROOM

NOTHING IS MORE CENTRAL to Italian life than meal-

time. It isn't skipped, it isn't rushed, and it isn't taken in

anything less than the proper environment. Like many

aspects of modern life in Italy, customs pertaining to the

dining table trace their origins back to

the Renaissance. In particular, the ten-

dency for Italians to spend a long time at

the table echoes the days when the feast

was the setting for elaborate forms of

The Florence dining
room of Fiamma di San
Giuliano Ferragamo is
a model of refined
elegance. The table is
dressed in classic
white linen and set
handsomely with fine
porcelain, crystal, and
silver. Soft candlelight
creates a warm and
engaging atmosphere
for her guests.

A group of friends gather for a leisurely alfresco lunch on a summer afternoon in Umbria. They are sipping local white Orvieto Classico wine as they wait for the first course: a rice mold drizzled with a rich homemade sauce made with just picked tomatoes. ABOVE: Six-year-old Veronica finds an open lap. In Italy, children are always welcome at the table.

THE WEEKDAY FAMILY DINNER HAS BECOME
SOMETHING OF AN ENDANGERED SPECIES
UNDER THE PRESSURES OF MODERN LIFE.
HOW ABOUT TRYING TO RECLAIM LOST
GROUND BY SELECTING ONE WEEKDAY
EVENING THAT CAN BE CLEARED OF OUT-
SIDE COMMITMENTS, AND MAKING IT
"FAMILY DINNER NIGHT"?

entertainment. Tables were arranged in large U-shaped configurations, with diners seated along the outer side only to better view the comedies, ballets, and other diversions presented between courses.

LIFE AROUND
LA TAVOLA

Despite the pressures of modern life—mothers who work outside the home, nine-to-five jobs, busy school schedules—a significant number of Italian families manage to gather around *la tavola*, or the dining table, for both the midday and evening meal. Thus, for many Italians, the dining room carries associations of pleasant times and the security of family. "It was such a comforting constant in my life," recalls Laudomia Pucci. "No matter what else happened during the day, I always knew I would have my mother, my father, and my brother with me for lunch and dinner. Sometimes we were joined by friends or relatives, sometimes it was just the four of us—but it was an appointment we always kept with each other."

Because it is so infused with the spirit of the family, the dining room holds a formal place in the home and in the structure of daily life, yet its use never requires strict conformity to etiquette or "rules." Around the table, as in many aspects of Italian life, relaxed elegance is not an oxymoron. One can be surrounded by splendid porcelains, stemware, and linens, but the meal always unfolds with the ease and spontaneity of a summer picnic.

SETTING
THE TABLE

Italians appreciate beauty in every aspect of their lives, and the table is no exception. From linens to tablewares—even to the presentation of the food itself—everything must please the eye. Echoing the aesthetic preferences that characterize their interiors and fashion, a well-dressed table in Italy is a model of classic refinement, never overdone, never fussy, never out of balance with its environment.

TABLE LINENS

The vast majority of Italian tables are dressed simply in white linen. Only a single cloth is used, always impeccably woven, impeccably laundered, and impeccably pressed. Layering cloths, engineering complicated ballgown-type swagging, or using boldly patterned tablecloths has never gained wide acceptance in Italy. Rather, not surprising in the country of Frette, Pratesi, and other world-renowned manufacturers of exquisite linens, great pride is taken in the quality of the cloth itself. A considerable investment is made in the acquisition and maintenance of all household linens, especially linens for the table.

When selecting linens for the table, let simplicity and elegance be your guide. White or cream is always a good choice, and, depending on your budget, consider a plain over- or underweave, a damask, or a cloth embellished with cutwork or tone-on-tone embroidery, such as a monogram.

When evaluating the cost of a table linen, it is important to remember that, when well cared for, it can last for two generations or more. In fact, in Italy, an inherited *tovaglia*, perhaps displaying the handwork of a mother or grandmother, is a source of great pride. It is still customary for a young bride-to-be to assemble a trousseau of linens before marriage.

When an Italian table is dressed in a print-patterned cloth, it tends to be a classic English sprig-and-bud-style floral. Foreign influences and inspirations are indeed welcomed with open arms, even as they are adapted in a quintessentially Italian way. Thus, a botanical-print tablecloth that might look so cozy in an English tearoom will appear, by contrast, quite tailored when laid out upon a rectilinear dining table set with classic white porcelain, crisp white linen napkins, pretty glassware, and silver.

An exception to the general use of table linens is found when a table has a particularly attractive surface, such as beautiful marquetry inlay, fine-grained travertine, or even a thick slab of glass set upon an unusual base. In these cases, the tablecloth can be eliminated altogether, even when entertaining formally. Instead, try using place mats of fine linen or cotton, perhaps outlined with decorative stitching or cutwork, and team them with matching or coordinated napkins.

Most Italian tables are dressed simply in white linen. Here, the crisp white tablecloth, white porcelain, and clear crystal accentuate the clean lines of the table. The napkins are folded simply into a rectangle and placed flat to the right of the silverware.

SETTING YOUR WEEKDAY TABLE WITH A WHITE TABLECLOTH NEED NOT BE A DAUNTING TASK INVOLVING AGGRAVATION INDUCED BY SPILLS AND TRIPS TO THE DRY CLEANER. THANKS TO A BOUNTY OF NEW STAIN-REMOVING PRODUCTS, WHICH CAN BE APPLIED TO FABRICS UP TO SEVEN DAYS BEFORE WASH DAY, A COTTON DAMASK CLOTH CAN BE TOSSED IN THE MACHINE WHEN CONVENIENT AND, IF REMOVED PROMPTLY FROM THE DRYER, MAY NOT EVEN NEED THE TOUCH OF AN IRON.

THE
DINING
ROOM

91

RIGHT: In this elegant place setting on the Ferragamo table, a monogrammed white damask napkin, folded simply into a square, is placed to the right of the knife. The flatware is silver-and-vermeil. Clear crystal is used for the two wineglasses, and the water goblet is a delicate red.

TABLE SETTINGS

"Italians love to create a beautiful table," says Milan-based journalist Carlo Ducci. "Even as a bachelor who has not yet set up a house for a family, I own five different dinner services. I love to be able to react to whatever mood I am in when I set the table for my guests."

Italians adore both beautiful, fragile porcelains as well as hearty, robust ceramics, and many homes have at least three different sets of dinnerware. Remaining true to their preference for classics, Italians favor fine porcelains decorated in the traditional manner. Consider therefore patterns with small flowers or medallions on a white background, perhaps trimmed with a delicate gold rim. If you prefer a more contemporary look, there are many good options among the porcelains produced by the avant-garde studios in Milan.

Dining casually with family or friends presents the perfect occasion to enjoy Italy's spectacular handpainted ceramics. A wide range of colorful pottery varying in design according to the region in which it is produced is available in the United States. (See The Beauty of Ceramics, page 105.) Many Italians enjoy collecting patterns from all over the country, then mixing them together when they set the table. Often they simply center a shallow bowl on a dinner plate. The first course—a pasta, risotto, or soup—will be served in the bowl. Once the bowl is removed, the second course is served on the plate. If a cheese, salad, or dessert is taken, the appropriate plates will be brought to the table.

When Italians dine formally, the table is set with a service plate that is never removed during the meal. As each course is brought out, a new plate—porcelain, of course—will be placed on top of the service plate.

FLATWARE

We owe a debt to Italy for *la forchetta*— the fork. It was Catherine de Medici, from the great Florentine banking family of the Renaissance, who, when she married King Henri IV of France in 1560 (she was only 14!), introduced this handy little eating utensil to the French court. It took another 100 years or so for the fork to gain wide acceptance, apparently because it required some effort to master the art of eating with it gracefully.

For the average meal, the Italian table is set rather simply. One fork is placed to the left of the plate, tines up, as in the United States. If a pasta or risotto is to be served instead of a soup, a second fork will be placed alongside the first. A knife and soup spoon are positioned to the right of the plate, just as they are in America. If no soup is to be served, the spoon will be eliminated: in Italy a spoon is never used to "help" in the consumption of pasta. A small knife for cutting fruit is placed directly above the plate, its handle pointed

LEFT: A perfect example of Italian elegance: small delicate roses decorate the scalloped porcelain plates. Subtle fleur-de-lys motifs are woven into the white linen tablecloth, and the napkins are monogrammed in the traditional white on white. Because this is a formally set table, a small silver bread plate is placed to the upper left of the dinner plate.

to the right and blade facing toward the plate. A small fork for lifting the fruit is laid directly above the knife, tines facing up and handle to the left. Finally a small teaspoon will be placed above the fork, its handle pointing in the same direction as the knife. For a formal meal, all the silver needed for the entire meal is placed at each setting. Pieces will be removed as they are used for each course; no new pieces will be added.

Despite this description of table customs and expectations, the truth is that Italians simply don't obsess over the protocol of table settings. For all but the most elaborate of meals, you may find any arrangement of flatware that suits the food to be served or the whim of the person setting the table. For example, one commonplace exception to the "rules" is placing the pasta fork to the right of the plate because pasta, unlike meat or fish, is eaten with the fork in the right hand.

GLASSWARE

The Italian table is set with glasses in a manner similar to the American table. For most meals only one type of wine—either white or red—and bottled water are served. Thus the water goblet is placed to the left of the wineglass. For formal meals, up to three types of wine, plus an *aperitivo*, are served. The glasses for these are positioned from left to right, in order of their use, with the water goblet to the right, and over the center of the plate.

With the island of Murano, famed for its glassblowing, right off the coast of Venice, Italians have a spectacular range of artisanal glassware from which to choose. (See The Treasures of Murano, page 106.) While some purists prefer to set their table with clear crystal, many choose beautifully colored creations. If it appeals to you aesthetically, combine clear and colored styles at the same setting for a sparkling rainbow of glasses.

> FOR A MORE AUTHENTIC ITALIAN ATMOSPHERE, USE A CARAFE FOR BOTH THE WINE AND THE WATER SERVED AT YOUR TABLE. (ITALIANS WILL PUT THE WATER AND WINE BOTTLES ON THE TABLE AT ONLY THE MOST CASUAL MEALS.) WHEN SERVING MORE THAN SIX OR EIGHT PEOPLE (OFTEN THE CASE IN ITALY!), USE TWO OR THREE CARAFES OF WATER AND WINE, PLACED CONVENIENTLY SO THAT EVERYONE CAN BE SERVED EASILY. THE EXCEPTION IS FORMAL DINNERS WHERE THERE ARE NO SERVERS; THE WINE REMAINS IN ITS BOTTLE AND IS KEPT NEAR THE HOST, WHO WILL SEE TO IT THAT THE GLASSES OF HIS GUESTS ARE REFILLED AS NECESSARY.

Wine bottles are not placed on Italian tables, except for casual meals. Instead, carafes, like this beautifully etched crystal carafe, are used to serve wine and water. For this table set for ten people, four carafes are being used.

BRINDIAMO ALLA VITA! A **TOAST** TO LIFE

"No one grows old at the table," states a favorite Italian proverb. Perhaps this is why Italians love to relax around the table, savoring not only the food and wine but the company of loved ones. Friends join family often. In fact, in many Italian homes, it is not unusual to have dinner guests two or more times a week. "When an Italian invites you to dinner at his home, it is a very important act of friendship," says Alessandro Falassi. His sentiments are echoed by Laudomia Pucci: "When you feed someone, it is like a gift. You are offering something of yourself."

This expression of emotion and genuine concern for the well-being of the guest can be obscured against the backdrop of the gracious ease and flexibility with which Italians entertain. Receiving friends on an average of twice a week, Francesca Antinori, who runs the Florence-based Marchesi Antinori wine company with her husband and daughters, invests her efforts in creating a calm and welcoming environment for her friends. "After they have put in a full day, I care very much that everyone I invite into my home is able to really relax and have a good time."

Creating the right environment is something most Italians trust to their moods and instincts, especially when it comes to dressing the table. "I don't really have a regular way of doing things," says Fiamma di San Giuliano Ferragamo. "I set the table according to the season, the occasion, or the time I have. I might either put a beautiful object or a sculpture in the middle of the table, place several smaller objects on it, create some unusual flower arrangements, or even add some color with fresh fruit of the season, like bright red cherries, or with colored crystals or ceramics." Like di San Giuliano Ferragamo, interior designer Pierro Pinto listens to his moods, invests a lot of energy into setting a beautiful table, and relies on objects more than on grand arrangements of flowers. "I like to decorate the table with a variety of objects: silver shells or dishes, ostrich eggs, crystal— whatever strikes me at that moment."

And, of course, the food must be presented beautifully. Italians follow simple guidelines: the food must be uncomplicated, it must be visually appealing, and it must not be too heavy. One example is to serve a rice dish in a mold surrounded by fresh green herbs and a sauce; another is to arrange a pretty platter of grilled vegetables in a rainbow of colors; yet another is to present breaded veal scaloppine, grilled to a golden brown and garnished with ripe red tomatoes and fresh basil leaves.

Katherine Mondadori takes a moment out from preparing a flower arrangement to say hello to the family dog Petunia. The flowers will not be part of the table setting, but instead will be used to decorate the entry hall and living room.

The Italian penchant for socializing, their comfort with spontaneity, and the relative ease with which many popular dishes such as pasta and risotto can be adapted to feed more people all combine to create the quintessential Italian attitude toward entertaining—what we might call the room-for-one-more factor. As designer Cristiana Vannini laughingly says, "Unexpected guests are really no problem! We just put another plate on the table." Di San Giuliano Ferragamo adds that the unexpected guest is just a natural part of entertaining, unless, of course, one is speaking about a formal dinner that is planned in advance. "It often happens with close friends that the guests may suddenly become more numerous than expected, but it's fun to be easygoing and even to improvise at the last moment. In a way, it adds to the atmosphere."

When the number of guests grows to forty or more—a surprisingly common occurrence in Italy—dinner shifts from around the table to *in piedi*, "on the feet" or buffet style. Katherine Mondadori, known for the colorful parties given in her Milan town house, prefers this style of entertaining. "I'm a very social person, but I really don't like to go out much," she confesses. "I like all my friends to come over to see me." About twice a month she throws a party for fifty to eighty friends. The house is filled with candles and guests move easily from room to room, and into the garden when weather permits. The food is always easy to eat: tortellini, ravioli, meatballs, stuffed zucchini, and for dessert, small cakes. The ambiance is

clearly engaging. Guests arrive between nine and ten at night and, as Mondadori puts it, "They never go home. I have no idea how they get up the next day!"

The zest for hosting large gatherings of friends and family is a trademark of Italian hospitality. Florentine Rosanna Pezzati opens the family home to fifty friends and relatives every Christmas for their annual *tombola* game, which is the Italian version of bingo. Long tables are set up in the large entry hall, good food and wine are enjoyed, and the *festa* goes on well into the night. And the Italian version of American Super Bowl parties, where friends and neighbors assemble to watch big televised soccer matches, can easily grow so large that several screens must be set up so that everyone can follow the action. Asked if she was having a good time, one young fan replied, smiling, "Oh, yes— you know we Italians love big parties."

Brindiamo alla vita! Cheers to life!

RIGHT: Many Italian dishes, like the pasta being served at this alfresco luncheon, can be easily adapted to accommodate unexpected guests. BELOW: An intense concern for the comfort of the guest is a trademark of Italian hospitality. For winemaker Francesco Giuntini, that certainly includes selecting exactly the right Chianti to serve.

BELOW: Like many Italians, Francesca Antinori, pictured here with her daughters Alessia and Allegra, takes great joy in receiving her friends and often entertains two or three times a week.

How to SERVE Dinner

Italian meals are served in a series of modest, equally sized courses. The emphasis is on taste, not serving size; the rhythm and sequence of the courses ensures that no one ever feels too full.

The meal begins with an *antipasto*, which literally means "before the meal." Next comes the *primo piatto* (the first plate), then the *secondo piatto*, which is accompanied by *contorni*, or vegetables. The *formaggio*, or cheese, is presented as the fourth course, with or without *insalata*, or salad, and is followed by fruit or by *dolci*, the sweets, and finally by espresso. At a very elaborate meal, a *piatto di mezzo*—a half-course—may be inserted between the *primo* and *secondo*.

ANTIPASTO

Antipasti are hostess-friendly foods, as they are generally served at room temperature and may be made well ahead of time. The most popular of these are Tuscan *crostini,* little rounds of toast topped with various meat and vegetable spreads, and *bruschetta,* called *fettunta* in Tuscany, which is pictured above. It is prepared by toasting or grilling thick slices of hearty bread, rubbing the tops with garlic, drizzling them with extra virgin olive oil, and then smothering the bruschetta with chopped fresh tomatoes. A final touch of fresh basil is used as a garnish. Other favorites are figs wrapped in prosciutto, an assortment of sliced sausages, olives and grilled vegetables, or fresh melon with prosciutto. Most Italian family meals today, however, do not include an *antipasto* because, when followed by three or four courses, it is simply too much food for the average person to eat.

To bring the feeling of a formal dessert course to the table without bringing the extra calories that usually accompany it, adopt the Italian style of eating a fresh piece of fruit with a small knife and fork. For fruits like plums, peaches, and apricots, use the fork to steady the fruit and make one large cut from top to bottom, dividing it into two halves. Remove the pit with the knife blade and place on the edge of the plate. Then lay the fruit cut side down on the plate and cut it into two or three wedges depending on its size. If you are cutting into a particularly firm apple, you may use your fingers to steady the fruit on the first cut.

PRIMO PIATTO

The *primo piatto* is almost always one of four traditional dishes: pasta, risotto, polenta, a hominylike pudding made of cornmeal, or minestrone, a thick soup that typically includes vegetables. Pasta is sometimes served *in brodo,* in broth, in which case it is considered both a pasta and a soup. When Italians decide to eat lightly, the *primo piatto,* followed by a salad, and, of course, an espresso is all they might take. Most Italians will tell you that the *primo piatto* is their favorite part of the meal, and every family has at least a half-dozen favorite ways to prepare each of the four dishes. Here a risotto incorporates fresh vegetables. The beautiful color comes from the touch of saffron in the recipe.

SECONDO PIATTO

The "second plate" is what Americans would describe as the entrée, although the portion tends to be smaller than most Americans are accustomed to consume for their main dish. The base of this course is, by tradition, chicken, veal, lamb, rabbit, or beef; in coastal regions, the meat will be replaced by fish or crustaceans. Traditionally, the *contorni,* or vegetable accompaniments, were served on a separate plate, although today they are not. Salad can be served instead of a *contorni,* always on a separate plate. Here oven-roasted veal is surrounded by garden-fresh carrots sautéed in butter.

FORMAGGIO

A selection of Italian cheeses, such as a mild Taleggio, a hearty Gorgonzola, and a smooth Bel Paese, may be offered; or a single, fine cheese, such as an aged Parmesan, will be served. Included among the offerings here are Gorgonzola, Parmesan, and pecorino. Today, deferring to lighter eating patterns, the cheese course has been eliminated from most meals.

DOLCI

Italians usually finish their meals with fresh fruit, but on Sunday or on special occasions, they will indulge in *dolci,* a wide variety of cakes, custards, cream-filled pastry, or frozen desserts, of which they are very fond. In fact, when visiting a friend's home for dinner, the invitee will very often bring the host and hostess a favorite sweet. Here, a delicate and attractive fresh fruit tart of kiwi, raspberries, strawberries and blueberries is served.

Eating Out

When an Italian takes you on a tour of his home, he will no doubt proudly point out where the family dines outdoors, be it on the terrace, under the portico, pergola, or loggia, or in a garden. Much of Italy enjoys a mild climate at least nine months a year, and Italians take great pleasure in dining alfresco whenever possible. Even city dwellers often have a country home to which they can escape and enjoy the warm-weather months.

The personality of the country table, like the countryside, is more colorful and more relaxed than its urban counterpart. The table itself should be quite earthy and robust, constructed of heavy wood or stone. Expected to stand up to a variety of weather, the country table also serves as a stalwart workstation for all sorts of tasks: repotting plants, shelling peas, even maintaining the garden tools. And despite its rugged use, the table is often so intrinsically attractive that it remains uncovered for meals. Coarsely woven place mats are appealing and appropriate; Italians even use the rush matting disks that are found in olive presses. A tablecloth, however, is not out of place; be it a plain, colorful cotton, a floral print, or the always proper white linen, many Italians love to dress their table for outdoor meals.

The tableware is likewise attractively sturdy. Plates tend to be thick even when not crafted of ceramic, and they sport brightly colored patterns that reflect the traditional motifs of the regions in which they were created. When setting an out-

To make mealtime easier, consider using a *carrello*, or service trolley. The Italian hostess keeps this handy two-shelf cart at her elbow during the meal so that she may remain seated with her guests yet have everything she needs close at hand. On the top shelf, keep clean plates and flatware, fresh bread, olive oil, bottled water, wine, and anything else considered essential to the meal. On the lower shelf, place plates and flatware as they are cleared course by course.

RIGHT: The guests at this summer luncheon in Umbria will enjoy a delightful pairing of nature's bounty with white linen. Grape leaves from the pergola, dahlias from the garden, and bowls of fresh fruit have been used to decorate the table. INSET: The robust green glassware is a typical selection for alfresco dining and perfectly complements blue ceramic plates.

door table, consider using lively combinations of different patterns and then accent the plates with handblown glasses; the kind with bubbles embedded in the glass, such as those from Biot on the French Riviera, are especially attractive in green, blue, red, and golden honey. Gather some wildflowers or snip a few roses from the garden to place in a vase, or simply decorate the table with a colorful bowl of fruit. The priority is to maintain harmony with nature so the country table and the countryside blend seamlessly.

WHEN SETTING YOUR TABLE WITH POT-
TERYWARES, DON'T LIMIT YOUR SCOPE
TO JUST PLATES AND BOWLS. ADD TO
THE MIX SOME COLORFUL PITCHERS,
BOTH LARGE AND SMALL, TO SERVE
WATER OR ICED TEA. SMALL CARAFES
CAN BE USED FOR WINE AT EACH PLACE
SETTING AND ARE ALSO PERFECT CON-
TAINERS FOR OIL AND VINEGAR TO CRE-
ATE YOUR OWN SALAD DRESSING.

Under the shade of a pergola, this simple and colorful table is set for the midday meal. The owners have decided not to cover the smooth white lacquered table with a cloth. Cheerful butternut-hued plates are accented with green glassware.

THE BEAUTY OF
CERAMICS

The term *ceramica* describes a range of earthenware, from terra-cotta to porcelain. Although pottery and lead glazing have been documented since Roman times, it was not until the Renaissance and the accomplishments of Florentine sculptor Luca della Robbia that the creation of ceramics was transformed from a rustic craft into an art. Della Robbia, known for his colorful figures of cherubs surrounded by wreaths of fruit, experimented with new glazes to achieve a unique and innovative rainbow of colors. He also molded his clay to bring out a three-dimensional quality to what had been a smooth-surfaced two-dimensional form. His techniques redefined the craft, radically altering the manufacture and decoration of ceramics.

DERUTA

Today, when Italians speak of ceramics, they usually are not referring to della Robbia's style of glazing but to the earthenwares that the French call *faience*, named for the Italian town Faenza, which exported ceramics to the rest of Europe in the sixteenth century. They may also be speaking of the wares known as majolica, which take their inspiration from the brightly hued, highly stylized, lustrous ceramics transported from Spain and the Near East through the island of Majorca.

With a ready supply of clay, potters throughout Italy produce ceramics that exhibit the best features of both faience and majolica. These pieces reflect scenes from their daily life, elements of nature that inspire them, or their personal interpretations of the myths that have touched their lives. Over the years, villages have become known for their own particular version of these familiar and beloved motifs, and while not an exact science, one can see aspects of a community's personality reflected in the patterns created by its potters. In Umbrian villages like Orvieto, Deruta, and Gubbio, stylized paintings of birds, plants, and mythological beasts dominate. In the south of Italy, in Capri and Naples, for example, the ceramics take on a Mediterranean flavor, often being decorated with brightly colored lyrical patterns or simple patterns inspired by birds and other animals. One of the joys of collecting Italian ceramics (many pieces are exported to the United States) is to locate, identify, and mix together pottery from different villages.

The styles of Italian ceramics vary from village to village depending on the traditions and character of each community. Some of the more recognizable village styles are shown here.

GUBBIO

NAPLES

ORVIETO

THE
TREASURES
OF MURANO

Katherine Mondadori, a member of the family that runs the Milanese publishing empire of the same name, readily admits to her weakness for glass. Her pantry overflows with a dazzling collection of Italian wineglasses and champagne flutes in myriad colors and styles. "I think they are so beautiful," she says. "When I have guests over, I just select a bunch of glasses at random; the effect of mixing all the colors and shapes is mesmerizing." Italian glass, traditionally made by artisans in Venice, is indeed mesmerizing. Not only the glasses used for drinking, but also the vases, decanters, and sculptures are considered the most elegant and skillfully crafted in the world.

In many Italian households the most cherished wedding gift is a collection of vases and decanters from Venice, and more specifically, from the adjacent island of Murano. The craft of glassmaking was established in 982 A.D. on the mainland, but it is said the glasshouses with their powerful kilns were relocated to Murano in 1291 to avoid the possibility of fire in the city. Most Venetians, however, believe the move was engi-

TOP: Beautiful Venetian glass from the collection of Katherine Mondadori.
ABOVE: A collection of small perfume flasks sits on a ledge. The glass objects have to be cooled slowly in an annealing oven in order to prevent the breakage that can result from rapid temperature change.

hard work, stubbornness, and a fervent belief in the genius of Murano's twentieth-century artists, set about to rectify the situation. Together, they organized exhibits and catalogues, and authored three books highlighting the works of three major artists, Carlo Scarpa, Napoleone Martinuzzi, and Vittorio Zecchin. These artists, and a handful of others like Fulvio Bianconi and Arturo Biasutto, were influenced by Paolo Venini, the Milanese lawyer who pur-chased a local workshop in 1921 and there encouraged experimentation, ushering in a new era of design in Murano. One stunning technique to emerge was called *vetro a tessere*, a process of weaving together strips of glass to create fascinating and intensely colored mosaics. The Baroviers succeeded in bringing serious collectors to these contemporary masters and their work. Today, because of the Baroviers, the artistic merit of the full range of Murano glass is fully appreciated.

Artists often took their inspiration from the colors of nature and the celebration of the seasons, such as the work at top left, "Alga"—or Algae—by Tommaso Buzzi, or the jug at top right entitled "Primavera"— or Spring—by Ercole Barovier.

CLOCKWISE, FROM TOP LEFT: Anfora "Alga," Tommaso Buzzi, 1932–33; Brocca "Primavera," Ercole Barovier, 1929–30; "Grande Calice a Murrine," Vittorio Zecchin, 1914; "Elefanti Rossi," Ercole Barovier, 1933–34

ABOVE: Gallery owners
Marina and Marino
Barovier with Pippo.
RIGHT: These beauti-
ful, translucent glass
vases were designed
by Vittorio Zecchin
in 1922 and called
simply "Tre Vasi In
Vetro Trasparente."
The vases at left and
right are wonderful
examples of the
decorative effect
of handles.

REGIONAL
FLAVOR

THE GLORIOUS PASTS OF Rome, Venice, and Florence notwithstanding, the Italy we know today is younger than the United States, since the nation became united as a republic only in 1861. It existed for most of its history as a network of independent city-states, each with its own dialect, foods, customs, and to some degree, its own climate and geography. Thus, it is only natural that even today each region bears its own unique stamp.

The quintessential sturdy look of Tuscany is embodied in this handsome cabinet, decorated with hunting trophies, pewter, and blue-and-white Chinese porcelain.

TUSCANY AND UMBRIA

Solid and *earthbound* might be the first words one would choose to describe the look of Tuscan and Umbrian homes. In their timeless interiors, heavyset rustic furnishings of deep-hued carved walnut or oak are offset by walls of thick white stucco, robust beamed ceilings, and warm terra-cotta floors. The color palette of surfaces and fabrics is taken from the surrounding landscape: moss green, Chianti red, chestnut brown, and creamy beige, to cite a few.

Tuscan and Umbrian interiors reflect the tone of a life lived off the land. Decorations often relate either to the hunt for game or to agrarian life: a richly colored oil painting depicting hunting dogs, for example, might be prominently displayed in the sitting room or a pair of massive terra-cotta urns used previously for storing olive oil may stand to either side of the front door in an entry hall.

Many old farmhouses have been restored by city dwellers, thus the last thing they want to remember during their weekend retreats is a too-polished urban persona. In fact, the fixtures and appointments are often delightfully simple and rough hewn: a thick rope "railing" running up the staircase, cookware suspended from wrought iron spikes, or an old millstone put to use as an outdoor dining table all serve as perfect examples of the unpretentious flavor of the Tuscan and Umbrian home.

ABOVE: This country kitchen, while displaying more utensils in plain view than do many Italian kitchens, nevertheless projects a well-organized personality. Some elements typical of Italian kitchens are the travertine countertop, the ceramic tile chosen for the wall behind the sink, and the large wooden armoire, which is used to store tableware. RIGHT: An arched stucco wall frames the entrance to a Tuscan dining room. The room has a pleasing, earthy feel with its terra-cotta floor, rustic wooden furniture, and simple decorations. OVERLEAF: Light and space characterize this sitting room in Umbria. The exposed wood frame of the couch harmonizes well with the terra-cotta floor and adds to the feeling of natural materials in the room. The two chairs are slipcovered in simple heavy-weave white cotton.

VENICE

Venetian interiors sparkle with the lightness and grace of the water shimmering in her canals at sunset. They are unabashedly romantic and lyrical, an intoxicating mélange of the exotic influences of the Ottoman Empire and the refinement of eighteenth-century Europe.

The colors used in Venetian homes are rich and sumptuous without ever feeling heavy; gold, crimson, indigo, deep purple, and hunter green are a sampling of the saturated tones one finds here. The textiles used are equally elegant: silk damasks and brocades, Fortuny velvets, and Persian rugs, to name a few. Walls are upholstered, papered, or stenciled, and moldings and cornices are finely detailed. Ceilings may feature trompe l'oeil architectural motifs, or they may be frescoed with pastoral scenes. And everywhere, from the terrazzo floors to the fireplace, to the interior columns, if any, one sees the burnished elegance of marble.

The splendor of the Venetian interior is seen on its furnishings and appointments. Gilded rococo frames surround the artwork; Murano chandeliers are suspended from the ceilings; and curvilinear lacquerwork chairs flank alabaster-topped consoles. In short, Venice is the land of delicious, romantic excess.

Venice is famous for its luxurious interiors, appointed in richly colored silk damasks and velours. The scroll-back sofas bring a lyrical mood to this room, as does the delicate crystal chandelier made on the nearby island of Murano. *Photo by Darblay/Stylograph*

ABOVE: Venice is well known for the shimmering terrazzo floors that can be found in many of its homes. Terrazzo is made of crushed marble pieces and stucco. The floor is laid down in successive layers that are compacted and finally polished to a brilliant shine.
RIGHT: Ivy geraniums tumble from a second-floor balcony above a Venetian canal. Note the rich, golden color of the stucco and the window grilles inspired by Turkish designs. *Photo by Darblay/Stylograph*

THE **SEASIDE**

Lapped by the Mediterranean, Ionian, and Adriatic seas, Italy enjoys over 5,000 miles of coastline. It is, however, the Mediterranean resorts, such as Portofino, Capri, and Costa Smeralda, that have contributed most to Italy's image of "seaside style." Blessed with mild climates and bountiful fruits and flowers, Italy's seaside is often compared to Eden.

Seaside interiors reflect both landscape and lifestyle. Homes are relaxed, with clean white stucco walls, smooth glazed ceramic tile floors, and comfortable, unfussy furnishings. Colors range from coral, teal, and ochre to a dozen shades of blue. Textiles are casual and practical: rush matting adds a pleasing texture to the floor, weather-resistant canvas covers the chairs, and diaphanous white muslin is draped across bedroom windows.

A delightful characteristic of seaside houses is the seamless way in which the interior blends with the exterior. The ceramic tile floor of a dining room, for example, extends right out onto a large terrace, both offering sweeping views of the sea. Large double doors may open to connect a living room with a vine-shaded pergola, allowing cool sea breezes to drift through the house.

This gracious entrance is typical of the homes lining the coast of Porto Ercole. Beautiful wrought iron gates, ivy-lined walls of ochre, coral, or raspberry, and generously proportioned courtyards paved in stone or gravel are frequently seen. The same color palette may be used indoors—on ceramic floor tiles, for example, or with natural textiles, such as rush matting on cotton canvas.

OPPOSITE: Another variation on the color of seaside exteriors. Note how this soft creamy yellow is complemented by the deep pink of the oleander and the red and rose geraniums above.

LEFT: Along the Amalfi coast, many homes display beautifully decorated ceramic tiles, like the one here, to mark the street address.

BELOW: Bas-relief sculptures carved from marble are often inset into the exterior walls of the grand homes along Italy's seacoast. Here, cherubs holding a flower garland decorate a stucco wall on the Tuscany coast. This exterior wall is typical of the beautifully weathered shades of stucco that grace Italian homes. Faded shades such as ocher, coral, and dark raspberry are exquisitely set off by shutters painted in dark green.

MILAN

Milanese interiors celebrate the genius of that city's world-renowned designers and architects. They are as elegantly minimalist as an Armani evening gown, and as sleek and fresh as an Alessi stainless steel teapot. With vision, attention to detail, and an insistence on function as well as form, the apartments and town houses of Italy's most modern city are both sophisticated and sensual.

Furnishings have a lighter-than-air feeling created by their slender wooden or chrome frames, or by the use of modern materials such as slim steel tubing or industrial plastics. The frequent choice of glass as a material for tabletops and shelves enhances this lightness, as does the fact that neither tables nor upholstered pieces are generally skirted.

In their colors and textiles, Milanese interiors are subtle and sophisticated. Cream, muted gray-green, beige, and of course, the monochromes of white and black are among the most often used hues. Leather, suede, wool flannel, and tone-on-tone jacquards exemplify the quality of textile that is selected to dress the rigorously clean lines of these stunning dwellings.

A Milanese dining room represents minimalist design at its most elegant. The blond floor melts seamlessly into the lightly sponged walls. The table and chairs form the single focal point on the floor space, just as the large canvas is the only focal point on the walls. Windows are dressed with just a simple linen shade. Note the industrial feeling in the metal frames of the sliding glass door. *Photo by Brackman/Stylograph*

LEFT: Modern design strongly factors into this dining/living area. Two pendulum lamps are suspended over the white lacquer table, encircled by canvas and metal chairs. The floor is polished slate. The room feels clean, spare, and airy. The few touches of color in the paintings and in the flowers on the table are particularly dramatic against the backdrop of black, gray, and white. ABOVE: A sleek and clutterless counter is typical of Milanese kitchens. Note the clean lines of the white cabinet doors, which have no visible hardware. *Photo by Sancassani/Stylograph*

A FEW THOUGHTS
ON THE **GARDEN**

ABOVE: A terra-cotta urn once used to hold oil now makes a beautiful planter for ivy geranium. Note the pleasing effect created by the juxtaposition of colors; soft geranium pink, red impatiens and roses, green ivy, terra-cotta, and weathered yellow stucco. OPPOSITE: Red impatiens complement the delicate red roses that grow along the wrought iron railing of Villa Santa Cristina. Note the beautifully weathered yellow hue of the stucco wall.

"I promise to keep myself close to nature," began a fourteenth-century oath of investiture for members of a league dedicated to the local administration of the Chianti region. A respect and concern for nature was, and still is, a strong influence on the lives of the Italian people. For centuries, craftsmen have worked with the materials and colors indigenous to their regions when building their homes and their places of worship. The landscape, dotted by graceful stone towers and well-proportioned farmhouses, has been enhanced rather than diminished by the hand of man.

Although most Italians no longer live the agrarian life, they stay connected to nature through their enthusiasm for gardening. In the city, where space is limited, tiny gardens sprout on terraces, ledges, and windowsills. In the country, where there is room to spread out, gardens expand beyond flowers and herbs to include vegetables and perhaps a fruit tree or two.

The overwhelming mood of the garden, whether in the city or country, is one of exuberance. Encouraged by the gentle climate, bright pink and red ivy geraniums tumble from terra-cotta pots placed in window boxes and on balcony ledges. Climatis winds its way up fence posts and columns. Wisteria, bougainvillea, hyacinth, star jasmine, and other blooming climbers cling to walls, gates, and trellises. Rosebushes are a particular passion of many Italians and are given center stage within their gardens.

Creating the feeling of an Italian garden requires thinking in three dimensions. Planting is not restricted to a few colorful perennials or annuals in a flower bed. Instead, favorite specimens are intermingled and encouraged to grow up, grow out, and tumble over. Let your imagination seek the possibilities for your own garden: try tucking a few pots of impatiens in a shady corner; train a potato vine to climb along a fence; erect a wire ladder along a sunny exposure for star jasmine to scale; step-terrace two or three levels along a bank with stone walls and plant an herb garden within their embrace. And if your climate permits, plant citrus trees in large urns.

LEFT: A small herb garden grows outside the kitchen door of this restored farmhouse in Umbria. This type of fence, constructed of sturdy branches reinforced by X-shaped supports, is typical of this area. RIGHT: The classic figure of a fruit-filled urn creates a graceful accent for this swimming pool. FAR RIGHT: On the Antinori rooftop garden in Florence, a peaceful breakfast nook is sheltered by a large standing umbrella. Note the pink ivy geranium, a popular choice for gardens in Italy. BELOW RIGHT: Looking east, several terra-cotta pots line the ledge and a pair of loveseats are placed parallel to one another. BELOW: This rooftop terrace in Rome displays many of the quintessential elements of Italian gardens: terra-cotta tiles and urns, tumbling flowers, and wrought iron railings.

THE USE OF CERTAIN MATERIALS WILL GO A LONG WAY TOWARD BRINGING AN ITALIAN MOOD TO YOUR GARDEN. EMPHASIZE STONE, CLAY, AND WROUGHT IRON EVERYWHERE POSSIBLE; FOR EXAMPLE, POTS SHOULD BE TERRA-COTTA OR CERAMIC, FOOTPATHS SHOULD BE LAID OUT IN FLAGSTONE OR CRUSHED STONE, AND PATIOS SHOULD BE PAVED WITH TERRA-COTTA TILE. FOR STAIR RAILINGS AND GATES, THE BEST CHOICE IS ALWAYS WROUGHT IRON.

OF PORTICOES, PERGOLAS, AND LOGGIAS

Three indispensable structures serve the insatiable Italian appetite for time spent out of doors: the portico, the pergola, and the loggia.

The portico, which translates as "porch," is a structure covered by a solid roof that extends from the roofline of the house, and leads to a landscaped area. The portico dates back to the covered walks of monasteries and convents that allowed monks and nuns to continue their walking meditations around the courtyards in inclement weather. Later, porticoes leading into doorways were constructed to shelter a horse and carriage and allow people to enter a home without getting caught in the rain.

In the past century, with the renovation of so many old farmhouses, Italians have begun to live on the ground floor of their homes: these previously were reserved for livestock. Thus, the porticoes have been enlarged and extended to create areas where the family spends much of its time during the warm weather. Many porticoes are large enough to

Sofia DeBenedictis and her younger sister Daria take advantage of the cool shade under the pergola of their grandmother's home in Umbria. The columns of this pergola are made of brick, although wood and stone are popular choices. The trellis roof was constructed with a wire grid, threaded with slim bamboo reeds. Vines were then trained up the columns and onto the trellis.

encompass space for dining as well as areas for seating and cooking.

A pergola is similar to a portico, except that its roof is neither solid nor inclined. It has a flat roof fashioned from a trellis and supported by two or more columns of wood, stone, or brick. The trellis roof is usually constructed of a wire grid, threaded with slim bamboo reeds and then planted with vines that are set at the foot of each column and trained upward. Over a period of years, the vines fill in and provide cool shade during the warm summer months. A pergola usually runs the width or length of the house. It may also be freestanding, like an arbor, and situated in the garden.

A loggia is also similar to a portico except that it is not always located on the ground floor, and it also tends to be smaller. In many buildings, particularly older apartment buildings, the roof extends another ten feet or more past the outer wall of the dwelling to create a loggia, thus serving to protect the balcony from rain and to provide shade during periods of full sun. Many families furnish the loggia with comfortable seating and a table for outdoor dining.

A portico, or porch, is a solid-roofed structure extending from the roofline of the house. Typically, the family uses the area for dining and relaxing.

THE
KITCHEN

THE THOUGHT OF AN ITALIAN KITCHEN conjures up images of a pleasingly plump grandmotherly type stirring huge pots of rich *bolognese* sauce while heady scents of garlic and onion fill the air. It is a warm, homey, and thoroughly inviting picture. It is also only half the story. Today, instead of holding dominion over a quaintly charming kitchen, *la signora* is probably standing in a room so sleek it could be a testing laboratory.

In addition to the requisite stovetop moka pot, this kitchen displays many of the elements often found in Italian kitchens, including granite countertops and tiled walls.

ABOVE: A *scolapiatti*, mounted over the sink, allows dishes to drain out of sight. BELOW: Schiffini's Box One System keeps kitchen supplies well organized and accessible. (SEE RESOURCES.)

Italians take great pride in maintaining their kitchens as paragons of order and cleanliness. Every detail is considered and the standing command is *tutto a posto*: everything in its place. Open any cabinet door to reveal plates, cups, saucers, bowls, and more, stacked with military precision. Everything is organized by type and size, and logically placed to allow easiest access to those things used most frequently.

To meet their exacting standards, and in keeping with their focus on the "bones" of a home, Italians will invest in the best kitchen appliances they can afford. They will also seek out brilliantly engineered storage systems; manufacturers such as Boffi, Scavolini, and Schiffini specialize in designing these ingenious systems.

For example, to clean up quickly after a morning cup of coffee or a light meal, many Italian homes have a small cabinet called a *scolapiatti* above the sink. Constructed with a mesh bottom, it has pull-out dish racks and a small plastic basket for silverware. Saucers, cups, small pans, and utensils can be quickly rinsed and set to drain in the *scolapiatti*. While the cabinet doors conceal everything, plenty of air circulates to let the dishes dry by themselves. Also popular are drawer systems specially fitted to hold cutlery, organize large utensils, and provide easy access to cookware.

In the Italian kitchen, equal emphasis is put on form and function. Although Italians have a strong preference for kitchens with the sleek contours of a racing car, they reject form for form's sake only. It is important that every design have a role in making the kitchen a more

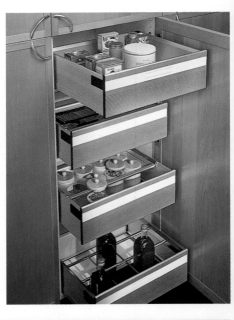

OPPOSITE: Dishes are carefully organized by size and type on the shelves of an antique armoire. BELOW: Architect Riccardo Caracciolo created a wine rack using a series of rounded terra-cotta pipes.

smoothly functioning place. After all, it is not worth concealing something if this ultimately makes it too difficult to reach.

In an effort to keep their kitchens free of clutter, Italians focus on creating as much storage as possible within an allotted space. For example, fruits and vegetables that should not be refrigerated are stored in a *portaverdure* rather than allowed to take up precious space upon the counter. A *portaverdure* is a small metal or wood box, often constructed with wheels and a couple of shelves, that rests on a balcony or porch outside the kitchen. Rolling the *portaverdure* into the kitchen when necessary is a simple matter.

Another common storage solution is to make efficient use of the eighteen inches or more of floor space in front of a partition wall. It is converted into a floor-to-ceiling pantry or *ripostiglio. Allora, tutto a posto.*

No Place to Hide

Architect Alessandro Corsini muses about his dream kitchen. "I would love to encapsulate the whole kitchen in sheet metal," he says, "to fit it out like a sleek glove, from kickplate to cooking surface." Although many Italians might substitute polished teak, marble, travertine, or white ceramic tile for the sheet metal, Corsini's statement sums up the collective Italian ideal.

At first glance, this might appear to describe yet again the Italian penchant for smooth, polished surfaces. But in fact, it is the value Italians put on cleanliness that

drives their image of the ideal kitchen. In *la cucina*, there must be no place for dirt to hide. White groutless ceramic tile floors, seamless stainless steel drainboards with integral sinks, smooth-planed cabinet doors: not one of these offers a cranny where soil can gather. Similarly, clutter-free counters and plenty of concealed storage prevent dust from collecting.

Virtually every aspect of the Italian kitchen can be seen in the context of a material that is both easy to clean and that won't obscure dirt. In Italy, out of sight is *not* out of mind! Most Italian kitchens are furnished in white or light colors. Counters are generally constructed of ceramic tile, travertine, wood, or, if budgets permit, polished granite or marble. Backsplashes are made of ceramic tile or stainless steel; floors are clad in terra-cotta or ceramic tile, or, less frequently, wood. These materials are all durable and easy to maintain.

FOR A SPIC-AND-SPAN KITCHEN, CONSIDER USING SOME OF THE CLEANING METHODS OF ITALIAN HOUSEKEEPERS. TO KEEP STAINLESS STEEL SINKS AND STOVETOPS SPARKLING, PASS OVER THE CLEAN SURFACE WITH A COTTON PAD LIGHTLY DAMPENED WITH RUBBING ALCOHOL. TO FRESHEN AND CLEAN THE BURNERS ON THE STOVE, RUB VIGOROUSLY WITH A HALF LEMON WRAPPED IN CHEESECLOTH. TO REMOVE STAINS FROM A LIGHT-COLORED ENAMELED SAUCEPAN OR CASSEROLE, FILL ALMOST TO THE TOP WITH WATER, ADD A TABLESPOON OF BLEACH, AND BRING THE SOLUTION TO A BOIL FOR FOUR OR FIVE MINUTES. WASH THOROUGHLY TO REMOVE THE ODOR OF BLEACH; RINSE WELL.

White is the most popular choice of color in Italian kitchens. Note the prevailing sense of smoothness here: the drawer pulls are unobtrusive, and only a few appliances and containers are placed on the countertop. *Photo by Sancassani/Stylograph*

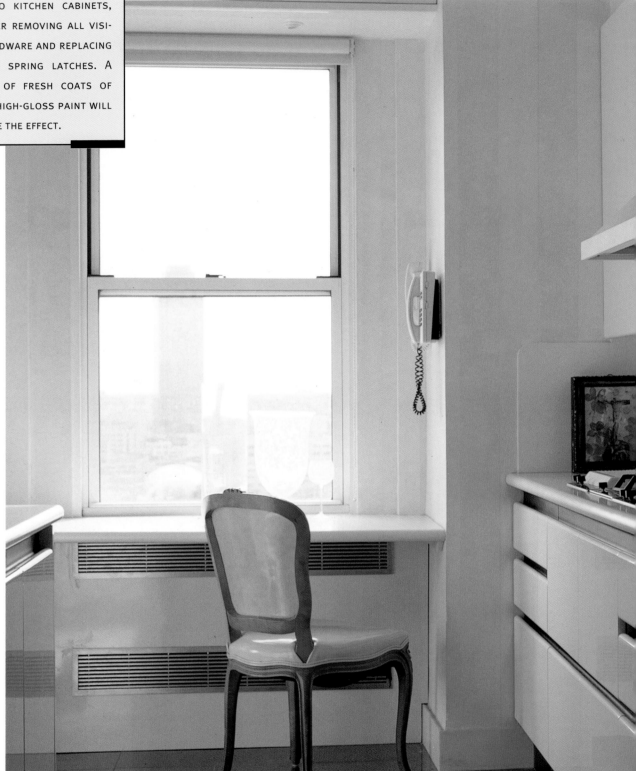

TO BRING A SLEEK, ELEGANT
LOOK TO KITCHEN CABINETS,
CONSIDER REMOVING ALL VISI-
BLE HARDWARE AND REPLACING
IT WITH SPRING LATCHES. A
COUPLE OF FRESH COATS OF
WHITE, HIGH-GLOSS PAINT WILL
ENHANCE THE EFFECT.

This New York kitchen, designed by Alessandro Corsini, describes the ideal for many Italians—no visible hardware, hinged covers to hide burners, and plenty of well-designed drawers and cabinets to keep equipment out of view. *Photos by I. Terestchenko*

THE WARMTH OF
TERRA-COTTA

Terra-cotta is the material equivalent of comfort food. Warm, rosy-hued, and enduring, it adds a reassuring glow to home and garden. It is also a useful material: foods cooked in terra-cotta casseroles emerge from the oven irresistibly moist and flavorful; plants thrive in terra-cotta pots; and floors covered with terra-cotta tile may survive for centuries.

The Italians have as many uses for terra-cotta as they do for olive oil. But, like the culinary classic, all terra-cotta is not created equal. Terra-cotta—literally, "cooked earth"—is an organic product, and thus depends to a large degree on the intrinsic qualities of the clay from which it is made. The best clay falls within a specific range of plasticity, neither too stiff nor too elastic. It must contain no more than 10 percent calcium carbonate and must be entirely free of calcium sulfate.

The way the clay is handled after being extracted from the ground also determines the final quality of the terra-cotta. After being washed to rid it of pebbles and other debris, and being mixed into a workable paste—all processes that can be mechanized with no ill effect on the final quality—the clay should then be worked by hand to achieve the proper density for the end product. If the clay is too porous, it will be less durable. This is particularly critical in areas with cold winters; if terra-cotta absorbs too much water, it can crack when the temperature dips below freezing.

The color of terra-cotta can vary widely, from a dark red brick to a sunny orange-yellow, depending upon the type of furnace that bakes the clay and the intensity of its heat: the hotter the fire, the yellower the terra-cotta will become. A methane gas–fired oven will produce an even color, while a wood-burning furnace, which fluctuates in temperature, will produce subtle gradations in tone. A fine-quality terra-cotta can be fired in either type of furnace, as long as it is adequately baked and allowed to cool slowly.

Terra-cotta floor tiles exhibit a variety of surface textures due to the process used while the tiles are undergoing their first drying. If they are placed upon a layer of sand to dry, for example, they will take on a subtle texture that varies with the fineness or coarseness of the sand. Bricks can be left as is once they emerge from the oven, or they can be polished, glazed, decorated, or treated with a chemical sealant. Caution should be exercised, however, when considering a floor tile that has been treated with a sealant, because it may be vulnerable to cracking and peeling.

When evaluating terra-cotta, ask if it was made artisanally or by machine. Examine the surface: is it consistent and free from cracks? Weigh it in your hand: does it feel substantial, or flimsy? With help from a good dealer and a little knowledge, you can ensure you are getting a terra-cotta that will serve you well for years.

ABOVE: This large terra-cotta urn, called an *orcio,* was originally used to store olive oil. RIGHT: When Shirley Caracciolo's children were young, she commissioned a local artisan to sculpt their likenesses in terra-cotta. They are playfully positioned on the porch and enveloped all summer long with bright ivy geranium. INSET: Terra-cotta tiles can be made and installed in myriad forms for floors. Here, rectangular tiles are laid to a very pleasing effect in a herringbone pattern. This type of floor can easily last over two centuries.

HOW **TERRA-COTTA** TILES ARE MADE

In the small Umbrian village of Castel Viscardo, an area blessed with deposits of flawless clay, Vincenzo Anastasio Sugaroni and a small team of skilled craftsmen work year-round producing handcrafted terra-cotta tiles. Every tile or brick comes with a guarantee and every customer is warmly invited to tour the factory. Sugaroni even welcomes local schoolchildren so that they may learn why his craft, handed down centuries ago from the Etruscans, is so important to preserve.

I met with Sugaroni early one Saturday morning for the grand tour. The tile-making process begins with the excavation of clay, which is smashed into small, homogeneous pellets and transported to a covered area until ready for use (**1**).

The clay is then compacted, washed, and taken by conveyor to the main working area, where it is diluted slightly in a mixing machine to smooth it out and make it more malleable (**2**). A portion of the clay is scooped out onto the worktable, where the craftsmen will begin to work it by hand (**3**).

Both the wooden mold used to form the tile or brick and the work surface are dusted with a fine sand to prevent the clay from adhering. After kneading the clay, the craftsman presses a small amount into the mold and removes any excess by passing a level over the surface (**4, 5**).

The molded brick is turned out onto a section of the floor, also dusted with fine sand, where it undergoes the first phase of drying (**6**).

While the bricks are settling and drying, they are turned once and trimmed of any clay that might have seeped out past the margins.

After a few days, the bricks are gathered into groups of six, eight, or ten and turned on their edges to begin the final phase of drying before being fired (**7**).

Sugaroni's large kiln can be loaded with up to 50,000 bricks. These are stacked in varying positions to permit the even circulation of heat as well as the escape of built-up vapor (**8**). The temperature of the oven is raised to 1,000° C for two days to fire the bricks. Craftsmen monitor the bricks' color from observation holes above the kiln. The oven is allowed to cool slowly, then the bricks are removed and readied for shipping.

The small village of Castel Viscardo is blessed with deposits of flawless clay, which is excavated and made into top-quality terra-cotta tiles and bricks.

1

MANGIA BENE!
FOOD
&WINE

"GREAT FOOD," SAYS cookbook author Giuliano Bugialli, "is food you could eat every day for six months and still be just as enthusiastic about it." In Bugialli's view, it is the simplicity and intrinsic quality of a dish that makes it so appealing, whether it's a plate of *bruschetta* made with perfectly ripe tomatoes and drizzled with deep green olive oil from the hills of Tuscany, or a steaming bowl of

A mouthwatering array of Italian specialties is set upon a table fashioned from an old grinding stone.

risotto topped with tender asparagus tips. Just as Italian decor emphasizes the proper appreciation of a few beautifully made objects, Italian cuisine puts the emphasis on a small number of wonderful ingredients, each of which can be tasted and enjoyed on its own merit, but each of which can also blend harmoniously with the others.

A survey of the fundamental building blocks of Italian cuisine reveals the pleasures to be had from these classic staples.

IL **PANE**

Few things symbolize the Italian gift for appreciating daily life as eloquently as a simple loaf of bread. Italians revere their bread; in fact, in Sicily bread is used to decorate the altar for certain religious ceremonies. Bread is never thrown away; in Italy, a huge repertoire of familiar and favorite dishes is based on the use of stale bread: *panzanella*, a bread salad; *pappa al pomodoro*, a bread and tomato soup; *miascia*, a bread pudding; and *crostini*, rounds of toast topped with various spreads, are just four examples.

Bread is served at least twice a day in Italy, with lunch and dinner. It is always sliced before being brought to the table and it is never served with butter. Bread is not put on the dinner plate, but instead placed on the tablecloth to the left of the plate, where it remains throughout the meal until the fruit or *dolci* are brought to the table. Bread is replenished frequently and crumbs ignored. Occasionally, at formal dinners, a small bread plate may be provided for the bread; it is placed just to the left of the dinner plate.

Many years ago, each area of Italy baked its own distinct variety of bread: the saltless breads of Tuscany, the flatbreads of Sardinia, and the skinny breadsticks, or *grissini*, from Turin are just a few. Today, the bread frontiers have all but vanished and the great regional specialties are enjoyed throughout the country. In America, thanks to the rising popularity of Italian bakeries such as San Francisco–based *Il Fornaio* (which means The Baker), these breads are becoming widely available in the United States. The variations of bread are endless and delicious. An entire book could easily be devoted to describing each type. The seven varieties identified here are among the most popular, but it is well worthwhile to seek out the nearest baker of Italian bread and do some tasty exploring on your own. Or, if you would like to try baking Italian bread in your own kitchen, two books to consider are *The Complete Book of Italian Bread* by Carol Field and *The Il Fornaio Baking Book* by Franco Galli.

FOCACCIA

(foh-KACH-cha) This bread is the inspiration for what is called deep-dish pizza in the United States. Made from unbleached flour and olive oil, it comes in rectangular shapes and can be topped with olives, onions, tomatoes, herbs, and more.

NAMES OF ITALIAN BREADS AND OTHER FOODS CAN BE CONFUSING DUE TO THE WAY THINGS ARE MADE PLURAL OR IDENTIFIED AS BEING OF A SMALLER SIZE IN THE ITALIAN LANGUAGE. THUS A VERY THIN *SCHIACCIATA* IS CALLED *SCHIACCIATINA*. *PANE* IN A SMALLER SIZE IS CALLED *PANINI*. *PASTO*, ONE MEAL, BECOMES *PASTI*, TWO OR MORE MEALS. JUST STAY FOCUSED ON THE ROOT OF THE WORD AND LET YOUR TASTE BUDS BE YOUR GUIDE!

CIABATTA

(tcha-BAHT-ta) The name means "slipper" and refers to the shape of the loaf. Made from unbleached flour, water, and salt, *ciabatta* is a crusty, rustic bread with a flour-dusted surface; it is fat-free. *Ciabatta* comes in different sizes; *ciabattine* describes the half-loaf and roll-sized versions.

PAGNOTTA

(pan-YOHT-ta) This is a robust peasant loaf with a hard crust and doughy center. Although it is made from an oil-free dough, the loaf will keep for two or three days. The top of the loaf pictured has been scored at the bakery, but *pagnotta* is also found unscored.

GRISSINI

(grees-SEE-nee) These breadsticks come in many different flavors and sizes. Some of the most popular contain olives, garlic, or onion. Delightfully crunchy, these breads are wonderful as additions to the bread served at the table, or wrapped with prosciutto as appetizers.

MICHETTA

(mee-KET-ta) This light, crusty bread makes a perfect dinner roll. The dough, like that used for *ciabatta*, is made from unbleached flour, but the roll is then scored on the top to give it its characteristic starburst pattern.

STIRATO OLIVE

(steer-AT-toh oh-LEE-vay) This is an olive bread. *Stirato* means "stretched," which refers to the shape of the loaf. It is a dense, flavorful loaf, made with unbleached flour, olive oil, and, of course, olives.

SCHIACCIATA

(skee-ah-CHAT-tah) This thin, crispy flatbread from Tuscany contains olive oil and is often flavored with herbs such as rosemary and sage. Like *grissini*, it is a delightful addition to the breadbasket, but it is also quite tasty topped with cheese and toasted as an appetizer.

DON'T CUT THE **SPAGHETTI!**

TEN QUICK TIPS FOR MAKING AND EATING PASTA

Giuliano Bugialli prepares spaghetti in his Florence kitchen.

1. Cook pasta in a large, deep stockpot. Pasta needs to boil in an abundant amount of water so that it will move around freely and not stick together.

2. Do not add oil to the water.

3. When the water boils, add coarse salt. Experiment with the quantity of salt you put in the water as it will affect the taste of the pasta.

4. Do not rinse the cooked pasta; this will adversely affect the surface texture by making it rubbery.

5. Don't rely entirely on the cooking time listed on the packaging. Instead, test the pasta to see if it is done to your particular taste. Remove a piece of pasta from the water and bite into it. How does the consistency feel? Italians prefer a firm, al dente pasta.

6. Do not break long pieces of pasta such as spaghetti. If it won't fit in one pot, use another, larger one.

7. Never precook pasta partway in the interest of saving time. It will just get soggy and sticky.

8. Italians never use knives when eating pasta. If you must cut a piece of pasta—a ravioli, for example—use the side of your fork to do so.

9. Italians consider pasta a course in itself and so it is always served on its own plate.

10. Don't believe claims that fresh pasta is better than dried. The quality of the wheat determines the quality of the pasta. For dry pasta, this should be a hard-grain semolina.

ORCHIETTE

FARFALLE

CAPELLINI

SPAGHETTI

PENNE

ORZO

LINGUINE

CHIOCCIOLE

FUSILLI

ZITI

FOR THE LOVE OF
PASTA

"I could eat *pasta pomodoro*—pasta with tomato sauce—365 days a year," laughs Francesca Antinori. "I never get tired of it." Far from it being a cliché, Italians adore their pasta, and most in fact do eat pasta in some form every day.

The word *pasta* simply means "paste"—in this case, a paste of flour, water, and sometimes egg. Pasta is enjoyed in myriad forms: *pasta in brodo*, cooked and served in a broth; *pastasciutta*, pasta cooked in water and then drained; *pasta al forno*, pasta cooked al dente, then layered into a casserole and baked in the oven. Pasta can be eaten hot or cold; it can be filled or topped with cheese, vegetables, fish, and meat. A nutritionist's dream food, pasta is low in fat, high in complex carbohydrates, and easy to prepare. With a light touch on the oil and cheese, it is as healthy as a food can be.

EATING SPAGHETTI THE ITALIAN WAY TAKES A LITTLE PRACTICE. PICK OUT A STRAND OR TWO WITH THE TINES OF YOUR FORK. WITH THE ENDS OF THE TINES PRESSED AGAINST THE BOTTOM OR SIDE OF YOUR DISH (NEVER USE A SPOON), TWIRL THE FORK UNTIL THE STRANDS ARE COMPLETELY ENTWINED AND ROLLED AROUND THE FORK. IF YOU FIND YOURSELF OUT IN PUBLIC BEFORE YOU'VE MASTERED THE TECHNIQUE, ORDER THE PENNE!

BUGIALLI KNOWS PASTA

As a young boy, Giuliano Bugialli was not allowed to cook. In his traditional Florentine family, the kitchen was the province of *la mamma, la nona,* and *le zie*—his mother, grandmother, and aunts. "But I always loved to be with them in the kitchen," he recollects, "to watch everything they did." Cooking is something that is in your blood, Bugialli believes, and clearly, it is in his.

A dedicated scholar on the subject of *la cucina autentica,* or authentic Italian cuisine, in 1972 Bugialli started his own cooking school in Florence, the first where nonprofessionals could come to learn more about traditional Italian food. Four years later, he opened a second school in New York. Bugialli has also written seven cookbooks, and has been honored both in Italy and the United States for his contributions to the art of Italian cooking, including Italy's prestigious *Caterina di Medici* award.

Sitting at the massive oak dining table in his Florence apartment, where his

Giuliano Bugialli is an expert on the subject of authentic Italian cuisine and runs cooking schools in both his native Tuscany and New York City.

students gather to taste the fruit of their labors, I asked Bugialli about a subject near and dear to his heart: *la pasta.*

CM: *How does one know what type of pasta to use: dried pasta versus fresh, egg pasta versus eggless pasta, and so forth?*

GB: It is a question of the sauce that you are using. As a general rule, the more robust the sauce—a heavy meat-based *bolognese,* for example—the more full-bodied the pasta must be to balance the dish. A full-bodied pasta, fresh or dried, is rolled to a greater thickness, includes more eggs (up to five eggs for six to eight servings of pasta), omits olive oil, and incorporates the coarser semolina flour into the dough. A light sauce, by contrast, such as one made from lightly sautéed fresh tomatoes, goes very well with a delicate, thinly cut pasta, such as ribbony *tagliarini.*

Beyond this general rule, many preferences have developed in regional dishes. With a classic Genoese pesto sauce, for example, the taste is considered best when it is absorbed into and clings to the surface of the pasta. Therefore, the dough is eggless, because it makes a more absorbent and sticky pasta. In Florence, some people even add a very thinly sliced potato to the water, which makes the surface of the pasta stickier.

Beyond the characteristics of the

dough, the shape of the pasta is also affected by the traditions of different regions, such as Genoa's *trenette*, or corkscrew-shaped pasta, used with the pesto sauce I just mentioned. In general, short pastas have cavities that cup the sauce so that it won't run off. Therefore, regional specialties aside, if you prefer to taste more of the sauce in every bite, you would select one of these.

CM: *Do you have any guidelines for composing a pasta dish?*

GB: The essential philosophy of Italian cooks is to establish a harmony between the various elements of a dish. We want to be able to taste all the ingredients. Take sauces, for example. If I want to take advantage of some perfectly ripe tomatoes in the garden, I will just barely sauté the tomatoes and then add just a leaf or two of basil after they come out of the pan. That's all. No cheese, because it would be too strong for the tomato. On the other hand, if it is winter and I'm making a sauce where I'm reducing the tomatoes and adding onion and garlic to intensify the flavor, it is a different story. In this instance I would use cheese so that the dish would stay in balance.

By the way, one thing I notice in America is that people put too much sauce on their pasta. You don't want to drown the pasta. The objective is to maintain a harmony between the pasta and the sauce; neither should ever dominate the flavor of the dish.

CM: *Are there any other misconceptions about pasta you see in the United States?*

GB: I recoil in horror when I see wait-ers assaulting people with grated cheese and ground pepper—as if you must take the cheese and pepper or there is something wrong with you. In truth, cheese is not used nearly as much on pasta as people think it is. It is not generally used with fish, game, or mushroom sauces because it fights too much with their flavors. It is rarely used in dishes with hot red pepper, which has too distinct a taste to coat with cheese. For the same reason, it is never used with the classic *aglio e oglio*—garlic and olive oil—combination. The problem with indiscriminately sprinkling cheese on everything is that eventually all dishes taste the same.

CM: *What are your favorite dishes?*

GB: I like to eat very simple things, simple preparations and combinations so that I can retain the freshness and flavor of the food. But when I say "simplicity," I do not necessarily mean "easiest." Simplicity takes a certain discipline, sophistication, and respect for food. You cannot be sloppy when you are trying to preserve the essential character of a beautifully ripened vegetable. You have to be careful in how you shop for it, how you handle it, and how you combine it with other ingredients. I have always admired a person who can make a simple dish with only a few ingredients combined to perfection as opposed to someone who comes up with a very complex concoction of fourteen things, which is ultimately so heavy and overdone it is not impressive at all.

Big CHEESES

Cheese holds pride of place on the Italian menu. In fact, given the choice between a cheese course and a dessert, most Italians will take the cheese. Cheese is also an important element in Italian cuisine; many pasta dishes would simply cease to exist without Parmesan, and *tiramisù* would hardly be the same without the creamy mascarpone cheese between its layers. To explore every cheese made in Italy would be a long (and delicious) endeavor but these four superstars will give you a solid foundation in *i formaggi*.

PARMESAN

Parmigiano Reggiano—or, more familiar to Americans, Parmesan—is the undisputed king of Italian cheeses. Hailing from Parma and Reggio nell'Emilia in the Emilia-Romagna region of northern Italy, Parmesan belongs to a category of hard cheese known as *grana*, or grained cheese, which was first developed by the Etruscans and made in large wheels suitable for travel. By law Parmesan must be made between the first of April and the eleventh of November. The stamp of the Parmigiano Reggiano consortium on its rind serves as your guarantee of authenticity. To achieve its characteristically sharp taste, Parmesan must be aged for at least two to four years.

Although Parmesan is best known in the United States as a cheese to grate over pasta, it is also regarded as a fine eating cheese in Italy. In fact, a slice of Parmesan from the soft inside portion of the wheel drizzled with a thread of fine olive oil is

considered a heavenly treat. When storing Parmesan, wrap it well in plastic or place in an airtight container in the refrigerator; it should keep for at least two months. The drier outer portion of the wheel is better for grating, which should always be done just before serving. Do not buy already grated Parmesan because it will lose too much of its flavor before you have a chance to eat it. Before serving Parmesan, grated or as an eating cheese, allow it to warm up from its refrigerated temperature for forty-five to sixty minutes.

PECORINO

Pecorino is cheese made from sheep's milk. It varies according to the aging process. Best known in the United States is an aged version of pecorino, known as Pecorino Romano. This cheese is stamped as such by the consortium in Rome, which controls its quality. Aged for at least eight months, Pecorino Romano is a hard cheese used for grating. It is sometimes mixed with Parmigiano Reggiano.

Another highly regarded form of pecorino is Pecorino Toscana, which, as the name suggests, comes from Tuscany. Regarded as a table cheese, Pecorino Toscana is aged only from three weeks to six months. It is light in color and semisoft, with a creamy, delicate taste. Unlike Pecorino Romano, which is made in big wheels, Pecorino Toscana is shaped into smaller convex forms. It should be allowed to warm to room temperature before serving—ideally with a perfectly ripe pear—and can be stored, well wrapped, in the refrigerator for weeks.

Sheep's milk ricotta is made from the whey removed during the making of pecorino. More rennet is added and the whey is reheated (ricotta means "recooked"). A second curd is formed, which is then put in perforated molds to drain. Because it does not come from the first curd, Italians do not consider ricotta a real cheese.

MOZZARELLA

Mozzarella belongs to a category of Italian cheeses called *pasta filata*, or "spun paste," meaning that the curd is literally spun into long threads before being shaped into a small ball. Mozzarella is a mild cheese and is often served melted—as in its familiar guise on pizzas in the United States—or breaded and deep-fried for a tasty appetizer.

The real cognoscenti consider only mozzarella made purely from buffalo's milk to be worthy of the name. This is rare now and most Italian firms produce a buffalo mozzarella that also contains cow's milk. For the finest buffalo mozzarella the key is protecting its *assoluta freschezza*—absolute freshness. Only twenty-four hours pass from the moment the just-collected milk arrives at the cheese factory to the departure of the cheese to the market. Needless to say, a cheese of this pedigree must be consumed immediately.

Good-quality buffalo mozzarella is available throughout the United States in specialty shops. It is sublime sliced and served with vine-ripened tomatoes, dappled with olive oil, and garnished with a few fresh basil leaves. It should be eaten as soon as possible after purchasing. If it

must be kept for more than a few hours, it should be wrapped in a damp cloth and kept in a cool spot. The refrigerator is too cold for its delicate flavor.

GORGONZOLA

This semisoft blue cheese from the Lombardy region of northern Italy near Milan is a favorite of Italian cooks both for their sauces and for stuffing pasta. Its light blue veins and strong earthy bouquet give it a distinctive flavor and thus afford it a special position on the cheese plate. Gorgonzola is virtually the only blue cheese widely accepted by Italians.

Gorgonzola does not have a crust, and is thus sold wrapped in foil. It is made in two varieties. One is less salty than the other and is labeled "*dolce*." This type is particularly good for cooking. Gorgonzola is sweeter and milder than other blue cheeses and should not be replaced with substitutes when preparing Italian dishes.

A good Gorgonzola will be quite smooth and moist, and should always be allowed to come to room temperature before serving. Because of its strong taste, it should have its own knife on the cheese platter. Wrapped well, it will keep for many weeks in the refrigerator.

WHEN COOKING WITH CHEESE YOU MAY WANT TO READJUST YOUR SEASONINGS. SOME CHEESES CONTAIN SALT, IN WHICH CASE YOU MAY NOT WANT TO ADD MUCH TO THE DISH ITSELF. SOME CHEESES HAVE SUCH A PARTICULAR FLAVOR, IT IS NICE TO ALLOW IT TO COME THROUGH BY TONING DOWN OTHER SPICES.

A Basic Guide to
Il Vino

Great wines have always been produced in Italy. Wine-making dynasties such as Antinori of Tuscany or Gaja of Piedmont have produced exceptional wines for generations and continue to do so. But the real story of Italian wine is what has transpired beyond her borders over the past twenty years. Italy is the largest wine-exporting country in the world and it holds the number-one ranking among imported wines in the United States. Unfortunately, until recently this was a distinction by quantity only: Italian wines were lackluster and characterized by inexpensive jugs of poor-quality Chianti. In the last decade, however, Italian wines have made spectacular strides in quality, winning prestigious awards and the approval of wine experts worldwide. The consensus among these experts is that Italian wines will continue their impressive rise and that the Piedmont in the north and the Tuscany region in the middle of the country are two particularly exciting areas to watch.

JUDGING ITALIAN WINES

A system of classification exists to help the consumer judge the quality of Italian wines. Wines that meet government guidelines carry the mark "DOC," or *Denominazione di Origine Controllata*. Wines meeting even more rigorous standards carry the marking "DOCG," or *Denominazione di Origine Controllata e Guarantita*, meaning the wine is not only grown and made under regulated condi-

tions, but that it is also guaranteed.

Although the system appears to create a logical standard by which to judge wines, it has been riddled with problems due to poor enforcement and insufficient designations. While a DOC or DOCG mark offers a reasonable assurance that the wine will be pleasant, a wine labeled *"Vino da Tavola"*—a table wine—might at times be even better. For example, Tignanello is a rich, well balanced, and internationally acclaimed wine made in the Chianti Classico district. It is not allowed, however, to carry anything more than the *Vino da Tavola* mark because no designation has ever been created for the combination of Bordeaux-style cabernet sauvignon grapes and Chianti-style sangiovese grapes from which it is made.

To address this problem, the Italian government is adding a new designation for the 1994 vintages onward: "IGT," or *Indicazioni Geografiche Tipiche*. Finer wines now carrying the *Vino da Tavola* distinction will be upgraded to either an IGT or a DOC classification. Until the new system is working smoothly, consider learning the names of a few dependable reds and whites from the most respected regions, or refer to an authority on the subject such as Burton Anderson, whose comprehensive volume *The Wine Atlas of Italy* is considered the standard text.

RIGHT: Chianti Riserva ages in oak barrels in the cellar of Badia a Passignano.

THE TAMING
OF THE **VINE**

Francesco Giuntini is the proprietor of Selvapiana, a winery in the Chianti Rufina region east of Florence.

Francesco Giuntini, the proprietor of Selvapiana, a vineyard based in the Chianti Rufina area just east of Florence, typifies the transition made by the current generation of Italian wine makers. "My great-great-grandfather, Michele Giuntini, bought Selvapiana in 1827," Giuntini says. "Since the Middle Ages, this property has been involved in the production of noble wines. My father died when I was quite young, and as his only son, I inherited the expectation that Selvapiana would remain one of the great wines of Tuscany."

For many frustrating years, however, Giuntini was not able to make wines of great quality. The family vineyards had been destroyed after World War II, and the new vines were initially pruned for quantity, not quality. "It took a long time to bring the situation back," he explains, "to prune the vines correctly for quality control. That took place by 1975, but it was not enough." Even if pruned for quality, in some years the vines produce so prolifically that the wine maker must thin the grapes. "We began thinning in 1987 and we've made great progress in the quality of our wine." Giuntini understates the situation. In 1993, *The Wine Spectator* named Selvapiana's "Chianti Rufina 1990" the best Italian wine and the eighth best worldwide.

WHITE WINES

Italians drink a great deal of white wine, particularly in the warm-weather months when the lighter varieties are served over ice. The light whites are best enjoyed as an aperitif, with light dishes, or with very spicy dishes that would overpower a fine wine. Northern Italy produces some sparkling white wines using the *méthode champenoise*, the traditional method followed by Champagne producers in France; the most famous of these by far is Asti Spumante.

LIGHT, EASY WHITES

TUSCANY

Galestro—*Very light; alcohol content cannot exceed 10.5 percent. Drink very cold.*

THE VENETO

Soave Classico—*Light, pale, and best drunk when young. Be careful with Soave. The name has been abused and placed on poor-quality jug wines. Make sure you are buying not just a Soave but a Soave Classico.*

LATIUM

Frascati—*Soft, with a touch of fruit, and very dry. Drink young.*

PIEDMONT

Gavi—*Light, with a hint of citrus. Fluctuates widely in quality so ask your wine merchant to recommend a producer. Drink young.*

UMBRIA

Orvieto Classico—*The finer version of the Orvieto DOC region, dry and light.*

FULLER-BODIED WHITES

Italy also makes some "serious" whites, fuller-bodied wines that are more complex in structure and can be favorably compared to the best whites coming from California or France. In fact, the northeastern corner of Italy known as Friuli-Venezia Giulia is considered to have a near-perfect climate for white wines. Quality can vary widely, so it is important to work with a knowledgeable wine merchant when selecting a full-bodied white. Some very good wines to consider:

UMBRIA

Cervaro della Sala or Burro della Sala— *From the estate of Castello della Sala. Smooth, well structured, aged in oak, these wines will age well.*

FRIULI-VENEZIA GIULIA

Puiatti—*Wines from this producer offer a superb selection of well-balanced whites fermented without the use of oak. These wines can be drunk young, but will also keep and age well. Consider the pinot bianco, which is flowery and crisp, with hints of apple; the pinot grigio, a rich, almost velvety wine; and the tocai, another rich wine with notes of hazelnut.*

PIEDMONT

Gaia & Rey and Rossj-Bass—*Two Chardonnay wines from the Gaja winery. These award-winning chardonnays are honey rich with spicy notes; they received glowing evaluations from The Wine Spectator in 1989 and continue to garner praise.*

RED WINES

Italy produces some superb red wines, wonderfully soft and velvety, that serve as great accompaniments to roasted meats. The most famous of these are the Brunello wines of Tuscany and the Barolo wines of Piedmont, which are on a par with the finest reds of Bordeaux. Most Italian red wines are robust and hearty, but the versatile, lighter reds of Italy are very pleasant too, especially when served slightly cool.

LIGHT REDS
THE VENETO

Valpolicella—*Light, smooth, and fruity. Don't confuse it with Recioto Amarone della Valpolicella, which is also a wonderful wine from this region, but certainly not a "light" red.*
Bardolino—*Light and very fruity. Best drunk when young. Serve chilled.*

PIEDMONT

Dolcetto—*Fruity, fragrant, and smooth, dolcetto is actually the name of the grape. Dolcetto d'Alba is the smoothest of the three varieties available; also available are Dolcetto d'Aqui and Dolcetto d'Asti.*

TUSCANY

Santa Cristina—*An easy-to-drink, soft, fruity wine. Because it is not too assertive, it combines well with food.*

MEDIUM REDS
TUSCANY

Tignanello—*A combination of sangiovese and cabernet sauvignon grapes. Smooth and rich, in its best vintages it has scored above fine Bordeaux wines in international competitions. This wine can age to a full-bodied red.*
Chianti Classico (Riserva)—*Chianti is* the most famous wine in Italy, and the Classico is the best variety. These are well-structured wines, solid but never heavy, with a character similar to a red Bordeaux. The Riserva distinction means that it has been aged for at least three years.
Chianti Rufina—*Rufina is a small zone northeast of Florence that falls outside the Classico boundaries. Some very nice Chianti with good aging potential is made there.*

PIEDMONT

Barbera—*Barbera is the type of grape that gives its name to this agreeable wine with fruity aromas. It can be drunk either young or aged into a full-bodied red. Best regions for Barbera are Alba and Asti.*

BIG REDS
PIEDMONT

Barolo—*Richly perfumed with fruit and full-bodied, Barolo is considered the greatest Italian wine. As it ages, its robust fruitiness mellows into an elegant wine. It is a perfect accompaniment to roasts and game meats. It is expensive but worth it.*
Barbaresco—*The neighbor of Barolo, this red is soft, velvety, and elegantly structured. It gets wonderfully smooth with age and, like Barolo, goes best with robustly flavored foods.*

TUSCANY

Brunello di Montalcino—*Traditionally the most acclaimed of the Tuscan reds, this is an intense, tannic wine. Slow to mature, it develops into a rich, full-bodied wine.*
Sassicaia—*Ranked among the finest cabernet sauvignons and compared to first-growth Bordeaux, Sassicaia debuted in the late 1970s and has become a classic. A deep, rich wine, with notes of black currant and vanilla.*

BALSAMIC
VINEGAR

The production of balsamic vinegar, the intense and aromatic version of wine vinegar made in the Emilia-Romagna region, is not a task for those lacking in patience: some of the finest examples of this dark, sweet condiment are matured for up to 100 years. Unlike most vinegars, which are made from wine, balsamic vinegar is made from the cooked "must," or juice that is drawn off the grapes and not allowed to ferment. Its name comes from the fact that up through the nineteenth century, this liquid was considered a cure for stomach ailments; extracted from plants, balsams are resinous substances that were used in medicine. Although most Italians regard balsamic vinegar as a wonderfully rich condiment, there are still those who drink a small amount each day as a preventive health measure.

The minimum age for a balsamic vinegar is ten years. Like wine, it is placed in wooden casks and blended with other vintages of the producer's vinegar. And, as with wine, the producer will periodically tap into the cask to sample the maturing brew, monitoring its progress and making adjustments. The longer it ages, the thicker and more intense the vinegar becomes; a fine balsamic will appear almost syruplike. Because it is so intensely flavored, balsamic vinegar is used sparingly.

RIGHT: Rich balsamic vinegar is drizzled over freshly grilled vegetables. OVERLEAF: A menagerie of bottles line an old ledge. Some of the vinegars date to 1885. *Photos by Bacchella/Speranza*

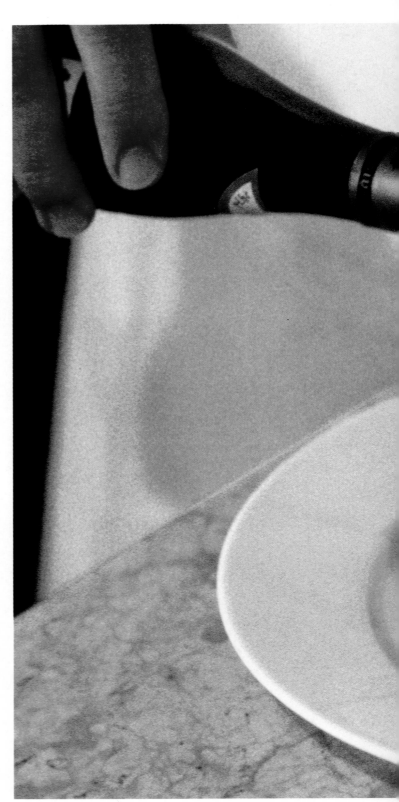

THE BEST BALSAMIC VINEGARS CAN BE VERY COSTLY. TO IMPROVE THE TASTE OF LESS EXPENSIVE (LESS AGED) BRANDS, MANY ITALIANS ADD A SMALL AMOUNT OF SUGAR TO THE VINEGAR. START WITH ABOUT ONE TEASPOON OF SUGAR TO EIGHT OUNCES OF VINEGAR, THEN ADJUST TO SUIT YOUR TASTE.

BELOW: A producer samples and monitors the maturing vinegar.
BOTTOM: Balsamic vinegar ages in wooden casks.

OLIVE OIL,
ITALY'S LIQUID GOLD

In Italy, people often pay more for a bottle of olive oil than for a bottle of wine. As far as purists are concerned, particularly purists from Tuscany, to consume anything other than the rich green-golden liquid that runs out from the first pressing of the olives—the extra virgin oil—is an insult to the palate.

The quality and taste of olive oil is affected both by the length of time olives are left on the trees and the method that is used for harvesting them. If they are left on the tree long enough, all olives will ripen, turn black, and fall to the ground; green olives are thus unripened olives, and they are less acidic and less fatty than the black. Since they must be handpicked, green olives also receive less bruising than do the ripe olives that often will fall to the ground. In Tuscany, legendary for the quality of its green-gold olive oil, olives are allowed to ripen only to the point where they will produce the best-quality oil.

After washing the olives, the first step in producing extra virgin olive oil (also called cold-pressed virgin olive oil) involves the grinding of the olives with large millstones. The resulting pulp is spread evenly over several large disks woven of coconut rope, reed, or a synthetic fiber; the disks are perforated with a central hole so that they may be stacked atop a spool set into a hydraulic press. The press squeezes the disks tightly together. The oil runoff, mixed with water,

flows from the disks, while the pulp remains trapped in the fibers. The oil is then separated from the water by centrifugal pressure.

The remaining pulp is generally sold to large manufacturers, who continue to extract as much oil as possible, first by using heat, and then by using acids. Thus, simply buying "olive oil from Italy" does not assure the quality of oil that comes from the first cold pressing.

Olive oil is viewed primarily as a condiment, something to drizzle over a plate of grilled vegetables or sliced ripe tomatoes. The idea is to be able to taste the oil, not to have it blend into and be masked by other ingredients. Even when used in cooking, extra virgin olive oil is added only in small quantities—usually just a few tablespoons. In other words, the initial purchase may be costly, but a little bit goes a long way.

ABOVE: A colorful platter of olives will be offered as hors d'oeuvres. All olives, if left on the tree long enough, will turn black, thus the green olives on the platter are unripened olives, which nevertheless have matured to a very agreeable flavor.
OPPOSITE: A carafe of green extra virgin olive oil from Tuscany is illuminated by the last rays of the setting sun. A bottle of olive oil of this quality is more expensive than a bottle of many Italian wines.

For a divine indulgence, deep-fry small wedges (not thin slices) of peeled potato in a quart of pure extra virgin olive oil preheated to about 375 degrees. Once the potatoes have started to cook, turn the heat down just slightly. After approximately twenty minutes (the exact time will vary according to the thickness of your wedges and the exact temperature of your oil), raise the heat again for just a minute to allow the potatoes to take on more color. The oil will not soak into the potatoes and the crust will be crispy, delicately flavored, and beautifully golden.

Brewing the Perfect Cup of Coffee

Once you've tasted the profoundly rich, smooth, dark espresso of Italy crowned with its *crema*—a long-lasting head of creamy brown foam—there is no going back. You have taken the first step on the same delicious lifetime addiction that binds Italians to their stovetop "moka" pots or drives them to coffee bars several times a day.

Whether consumed as espresso or in various other modes such as cappuccino, the first step in making an authentic Italian brew is choosing the right coffee. Italians like strong coffee—which should not be confused with acidic coffee. The arabica beans used in making espresso are imported largely from Ethiopia (where coffee originated before it was brought into Venice in the fifteenth century), as well as from other parts of Africa, Java, India, and Southeast Asia. The beans, which are a deep brown rather than black in hue, are roasted very slowly at low temperatures to avoid the acidity that results from quick roasting.

Ideally, coffee beans are ground at home; for espresso this should be to the consistency of fine sand or table salt.

If you don't have a grinder, you should buy only enough ground coffee to last the week, as it will not stay at peak freshness and flavor very long. It is important to remember that coffee beans are like wine grapes. The same bean in the hands of different producers can produce very different results. Experiment with different coffees from a specialty store until you find one that suits your palate. Two packaged brands of Italian coffee that are quite nice are Lavazza (the *crema e gusto* variety won high marks from many Italians I met) and Illy Espresso.

Unless the family owns an espresso machine—which is more often the province of the local coffee bar—espresso is made in the stovetop moka pot. Technically, this type of coffee is called moka, not espresso. The humble moka pot is as simple to use as it is dependable.

A real espresso machine, by contrast, uses either a piston or a pump to force water through the coffee grounds; hence, the name *espresso*, which means "pressed out." In the 1930s, Milanese coffee bar owner Achilles Gaggia devised a hand-operated piston pump to fortify the extraction pressure of the older steam-powered machines. His innovations added body and flavor to the then-unremarkable beverage and paved the way for a new generation of machines that provide the luxury of real espresso at home.

A stovetop moka pot is the most popular method of making coffee in the Italian home. The detachable bottom half is filled with cold water up to the mark of the small screw on the outside of the pot. The coffee holder is then filled with untamped grounds. The top is reattached and the pot is placed over moderate heat. As the temperature rises, the pressure forces the water up through the grounds and into the upper chamber. When you hear a gurgling noise, the coffee is ready.

WHEN MAKING COFFEE, TRY USING BOTTLED SPRING WATER (FLAT, NOT EFFERVESCENT) FOR THE BEST POSSIBLE RESULTS. ITALIANS DRINK COPIOUS AMOUNTS OF BOTTLED WATER, AND THEY ALSO USE IT TO MAKE COFFEE.

SIX GREAT WAYS
TO **DRINK COFFEE**

ESPRESSO: This is the foundation of all Italian coffees. A serving is just an ounce or two in a small cup. Purists drink it straight; many Italians, however, prefer to add a healthy spoonful of sugar. One doesn't linger over an espresso; it is quickly consumed at just the right temperature, not scalding, just pleasantly hot.

CAPPUCCINO: Cappuccino means "hood" and derives from the type of cowl worn by the Capuchin monks. In Italy, the drink is affectionately referred to as *cappucci*. Made with frothed milk, cappuccino combines one-third espresso, one-third steamed milk, one-third foam. Add sugar to taste.

CAFFE LATTE: *Latte* means "milk," and *caffe latte* is simply a mixture of espresso and steamed milk, with one-third espresso and two-thirds milk. It is most often served in a tall glass.

CAFFE MACCHIATO:
Macchiato means "stained" or "spotted," thus *caffe macchiato* is espresso colored with just a dash of foamed milk. Add sugar to taste.

CAFFE FREDDO: *Freddo* means "cold," and so *caffe freddo* is iced espresso. Once the espresso is brewed, it is quickly put into a martini shaker filled with ice and shaken vigorously. It is then poured into a pretty, long-stemmed glass to make a perfect summer treat.

CAFFE CORRETTO: Literally, this means "corrected coffee," which is the genteel way of asking for espresso laced with brandy, grappa, whiskey, or some other liquor.

THE **TIME** OF YOUR **LIFE**

Whether we live in Naples, Italy, or Naples, Florida, we are allotted twenty-four hours each day. How we choose to spend them, and our perception of how much or how little time we have, is a function of our culture. Bringing the feeling of Italy home goes beyond the decoration of a home or the preparation of food—it is about the way we view and use our time. During the making of this book, many of the Italians I met shared their views on this important subject. Here are a few of their thoughts.

"One of the great lessons of the Renaissance is to know yourself—to find your balance and your rhythm," says Alessandro Falassi. "Today with our faxes, computers, and satellites, we face a real danger of overheating our civilization. We can't always be on the go—batteries need to be recharged. It is important for us to remember that, although technology can be a wonderful servant, it can be a terrible master."

Commenting on the torrid pace that seems to have overtaken so many cities,

Laudomia Pucci puts it succinctly: "I don't understand all of this grabbing-a-sandwich-at-your-desk business. If you can't even find the time to stop and give yourself a proper lunch, what are you doing with your life?"

"City life presents us with so many distractions," says Francesco Giuntini, "we don't find enough time to simply sit and talk with each other. That is why it is so important to spend time in the country, close to nature, and enjoy a respite from the pace of the city."

"I don't really know what I'll be doing in the next five years, or the next ten years," says Giuliano Bugialli. "I live in the day, I enjoy what I'm doing, and I trust that life—with all its discoveries—will follow a natural course. I've never had a grand plan, yet look at all the wonderful things that have happened. Why would I start making plans now?"

Journalist Carlo Ducci has the final word: "I don't think it's very logical to get so caught up in making plans for tomorrow that you lose the pleasure of today."

Classic Italian Meals

Menu 1
(serves four)

Bruschetta with Fresh Tomato

Penne with Zucchini

Veal Cutlets with Sautéed Carrots

Strawberries with Mascarpone Cheese

Bruschetta with Fresh Tomato

4 to 6 plum tomatoes, chopped
2 large cloves garlic, 1 finely minced,
*   1 sliced in half*
2 tablespoons extra virgin olive oil
4 to 5 leaves fresh basil, chopped
Salt and pepper, to taste
4 large or 8 small slices coarse, crusty
*   bread (like a Tuscan bread or*
*   sourdough batard)*

Combine plum tomatoes, minced garlic, olive oil, chopped basil, and salt and pepper in a glass bowl. Set aside for about 30 minutes, stirring once or twice.

Toast or grill the bread slices, then rub with garlic halves.

Top with tomato mixture, drizzle with additional olive oil if desired, and serve immediately.

Penne with Zucchini

1 pound penne
2 medium-sized zucchini, sliced thin
Juice of 1 lemon plus zest of 1/2 lemon
2 cloves garlic, minced (or more to
*   taste)*
2 tablespoons extra virgin olive oil
Grated fresh parmesan (optional)

Prepare penne according to package directions.

Sauté garlic in olive oil just until lightly brown, then add sliced zucchini, lemon juice, and lemon zest. Turn down heat to medium and cover. Cook, stirring occasionally, for 4 to 5 minutes, or until zucchini has softened to preference.

Place penne in a large bowl, add sautéed zucchini, and toss. Serve immediately. Top with grated parmesan if desired.

Veal Cutlets

1/2 cup freshly grated parmesan cheese
1/2 cup seasoned bread crumbs
1 egg, beaten
4 boneless veal cutlets (about 1
*   pound total), pounded thin*
2 tablespoons extra virgin olive oil
1 tablespoon fresh squeezed lemon
*   juice*
1/4 cup white wine

Combine the cheese and bread crumbs on a plate. Put the beaten egg in a shallow dish. Dip cutlets in egg, then into the bread crumb/cheese mixture.

Heat the oil in a large skillet over medium-high heat. Sauté cutlets about 2 minutes on each side until they are golden brown.

Remove cutlets from skillet to a warmed platter. Add lemon juice and wine to skillet and reduce heat to medium. Scrape bottom of pan so that browned bits combine with liquids to make a sauce. Pour sauce over veal and serve.

Sautéed Carrots

6 to 7 medium carrots, sliced thin
1/4 cup butter
Salt and pepper, to taste

Melt butter in a large skillet over low-medium heat. Add carrot slices and cook until tender. Season to taste.

Strawberries with Mascarpone Cheese

1 pint fresh strawberries
Mascarpone cheese (available at
*   better food stores)*

Wash, hull, and slice the strawberries in half. Divide into four small bowls.

Top each serving with a dollop of mascarpone cheese.

INDEX